DATE DUE

JE 1 '00			

DEMCO 38-296

SIXTY SECONDS

AMS PRESS

NEW YORK

Sixty Seconds

by

MAXWELL
BODENHEIM

New **HL** *York*

HORACE LIVERIGHT

1929

blication Data

Reprint of the _____ by H. Liveright,
New York.
   I. Title.
PZ3.B6317Sil2   [PS3503.017]   813'.5'2   73-18549
ISBN 0-404-11364-8

Reprinted by arrangement with Liveright, New York, N. Y.

From the edition of 1929, New York
First AMS edition published in 1975
Manufactured in the United States of America

AMS PRESS INC.
NEW YORK, N. Y. 10003

DEDICATION IN VERSE

THE sunset nears its end—a drenching red
Upon the undecipherable
Innocence of low clouds,
Upon the sky's so matchless, blue,
Impersonal acquiescence.
Oh, if this far horizon did not stand
And light remained in one eternal morning,
There would be sunsets still of mind and heart,
For sunsets are but poetry
And pessimism, lending strength and softness
To the lives of human beings
Needing much to creep away
From all the broken promises of light.
Poetry and pessimism then,
Meeting in the line of understanding
Which must be every brooding man's horizon.
This scene is not an actual sun
That slipped below the shoulder of a hill
And left great flakes of apple-blossom red
To paint a cravenly untrue good-by.
This drenching red contains the blood
Of men who died upon the earth
In many mornings, afternoons,
And rise again to say that night is false:

To say it for a moment, in all
The ineffable pathos and frailness of their challenge,
Before the night swoops down again
And seems to end it, as it once
Seemed to end their breath and make them naught.
The moments never end, nor do the night's
Imaginary victories, and none
But poets hoping past the death of hope
Will dare to say that sunsets are more real
Than night and day, because sunsets alone
Can drench the swelling sky and make it find
Beauty too keen to live, too strong to die.

SIXTY SECONDS

SIXTY SECONDS

OH, let us leave metaphysical conjectures for a time! It may be indeed that Time is one of the dimensions in space. If a man could stand far apart from the earth, and if the light from his eyes could travel toward the earth quintillions of times faster than that light which makes our days and nights, then this man might be able to watch events that happened on the earth three or four hundred years ago. Yes, call this life of ours an impenetrable illusion, if you must, and yet believe that it is real and deep . . . deep . . . with moments of beauty too swiftly dangerous for human breath to catch their rhythms without hurrying into death, with moments of depression and blasphemous pessimism—the dark plowings without which light would be—what? A shallowly familiar monotone!

Let small critics, with their buttocks strapped to the hills of this earth, rail at the few children of rending darkness and call them garbage-venders, spenders of hatred and skillful ugliness. Let small critics, secretly terrified by the seeming viciousness and impermanence of life, cry out for sweetness, faith, wholesomeness, the insipid rodomontades of normality. They cannot help themselves—they are cowards, poor, struggling cowards, and without the drugs and bladders which they concoct so eagerly, so persistently, they would lie upon their beds some morning and feel no need ever to rise again.

John Musselman had escaped from this need—this clinging fright which makes men and women sing and paint every variety of consoling, elevating, ennobling lie and inflation. John Musselman was standing in one of the death-cells of a state-penitentiary and starting his last minute of life on earth. One minute later he would walk through the door of the cell and join the guards waiting to take him to the death-chamber, but a dead man would step from his cell. The real John Musselman, an invisible corpse, would remain within the cell, still standing there, still held up by the lightest stiffness of relinquished survival. The real John Musselman in the cell might then be compared to the arm of a soldier on a battlefield, rigidly held up in the gesture of deserted prayer and yet containing the smallest tincture of supplication to keep it from falling. In the meantime, the dead part of John would march to the death-room, with two guards striding before and behind this emptied Robot and with a minister walking at its side and still chanting biblical lines of crude hope, assertions of repentant purity . . . the clean, powerful, springy flesh of human beings pronounced unclean and evil . . . a noun and its adjective, sin and sinful, manufactured by spurious mystics almost two thousand years ago to make their mediocrity and their fleshly hesitations vindictive toward emotional curiosity and pagan-impulse, and yet to hide, oh, sonorously to hide, this vindictiveness beneath every assumption of benevolent restraint. . . .

The Robot would sit in the electric-chair, with an unreal smile on its face, like a glistening rubber-stamp. The little, funny, jerking steps would be over, and stillness would end the lie of animation. "Have you any last words to say?" Something deposited a phonograph in the breast of the Robot, where the absent heart once quivered and swayed . . . a few last words still to be played on the phonograph record. "I hope that life, some day, will be kinder to those . . . men . . . (did the needle catch in a bloodclot?) . . . those men . . . who are impulsive children. Good-by . . . good-by." . . . Then stern, shaken men—the unwilling flunkies of murderous retribution—would strap the Robot down and fasten the electrodes to its bare lower leg—so punily, removedly bare—and the black hood would be dropped over the poor, unrewarded, papiermâché face. . . . The body heaved upward in a convulsion? It was nothing—a last coiled spring in the Robot snapped by the electric current so that the creature, beyond repair, might be shipped back to the pulp factory of a waiting earth. And with the fracture of this last spring the real John Musselman, left behind in the cell, would fall down, would evaporate, and that incredible lingering which held it up—immortal soul, or final stubbornness of mind and heart—would die, or glide forth to substances and measurements beyond the perceptions of finite minds and senses.

But now, John Musselman, still utterly, keenly alive, was standing in the death-cell and starting his last minute of life on earth. The shaved top of his head, a grayish pink dome, gleamed in the half-eliminated morning light of the cell. When hair is clipped from a head, an essential sincerity shows itself openly on this head. The head becomes grotesque, blunt, independent. A hard dream of outline is then revealed in its strength, or weakness, or combination of both. The sensitively coquettish adornment of hair must ever obscure and subdue this dream-reality—for what are dreams but realities that refuse to fall asleep?—but all the subtly pliant, chestnut strands once growing on John's head had now been reduced to their stubbled roots and his head could no longer be mistaken, pardoned.

Broad, curving up only a little on the top, just separated from straightness by an arching inch at the back, and with a high, slightly receding front above the eyes, his head was that of a self-centered boy with some intelligence to make him less young, and some crucified emotion to make him less impulsive, but a boy nevertheless—an unashamed, vibrant, playing egotist, who had been ambushed, beaten down by a world of egotists more afraid of themselves, oh, much more intent upon deceiving themselves with the old, trite, sweetly sophistical erasures . . . the old claims and manufactured motives of kindness, good-will, fairness. . . . A potential saint, murderer, poet, flesh-stroker—they were all compressed not unfriendlily upon this head, for such distinctions are always partly false, partly exaggerated by the human need to worship, or hate, different ones among them, and they live within the breast and head of every individual, dormant for the most part but requiring only an overpowering tug of outside circumstance to bring them forth. Saint, murderer, poet, flesh-stroker—they are never really apart from each other, never more than opposite gestures made by one, punished, human *curiosity*.

John Musselman was a murderer about to die for his crime, and yet this past murder held within itself the elements of saintliness, wild poetry striking down an obstacle in its path, and flesh immersed only in its own self-destroying flare-up of nerves. John had the face of a man who knew that he had only one more minute to live—a face where pain had become a vestige of smoldering and where fear, yielding gravely to an inevitably immediate extinction, drew near to bravery. It must be indeed that pain changes men to monks or animals, yes, it must be so. The monk fingers his chain of beads and each bead becomes a vowel of pain between the consonants of his endurance: the animal finds that mind and soul are lies, that nothing remains save the abject writhings of flesh. John Musselman had squelched the animal to a few, involuntary tremors and had become the monk, not quite afraid of death . . . not quite able to welcome it . . . feeling not pure enough to die . . . wishing that he might shake off the mental dross within him before going to an adventure as exacting and athletic as death . . . praying that his heart and mind might assume no mere bravado of the caught animal but might walk to death with a clear, clean, buoyant inquisitiveness. . . .

The skin of John's face, once mild brown with ruddiness in it, had been turned by confinement to a whitish, grayish brown, so like the indescribable tint of once vigorous life in an even struggle with that anemia which is partly of the soul. John's eyes were large and black—that black where night concentrates her luminous hatred for the titterings, folderols, paucities, and unromantic industries of day; that black which holds the amazing, untender, mind-soaked poetry so disliked by men who wish their earth to boast, or sing itself to sleep; that black where adjectives of every kind slip into each other and repudiate the make-believe enmity solidified by nouns, prodded on by adverbs; that black where realism and fantasy are no longer ordinary in the first quality and grotesque in the second but deeply apologetic for the misunderstandings and cleavages forced upon them by men.

You, too, John Musselman, are apologetic. Your life held errors, hustling omissions, peacock-deliriums, and a little appalled by the lack of time in which to correct them now, you ask for a pardon from whatever force may stand behind life: ask for release from that unmoving, never-fully-justified *praise* and *blame* that men are always so eager to give each other. Be resigned, man, standing in a hideous box and waiting for an imminent death. If anything exists beyond the life which we hug so theatrically and with so many counterfeits of assurance—any surviving purpose, domain of al-tered identities, or power too thinly simple for human comprehension—it will be far apart from eulogies and condemnations, the twin *poisons* of earthly existence, and it will not be disposed to see any difference between murderer and Christ, communist and sultan, housewife and slut. Be sure of that, John Musselman —make it a super-armor for this, your last minute of life on earth. . . .

John's nose would have been straight but for a little hump in the middle of its downward slope; his lips were thick and slack—tired out from fights with thought and emotion; his face, which had grown through thirty-two years of life, was now that of a boy and an old man. They had fought against each other, this lad and dotard, but they were exhausted now, and having drawn apart to gaze at each other, they were inclined to wonder, oh, so intensely to wonder whether the old man had not always been hiding in the boy while the boy himself lurked within the graybeard: whether their opposition had not sprung from the fact that each one wanted to expel the other from himself. . . .

(Come on, you realists, shout: "This is idle phantasmagoria, euphuism lost in a maze of over-refinements," and then, to add a climax, frown at the "irrelevant discursiveness" of these sentences. The author is letting his readers behind the scenes, tearing off the bland veilings of a spurious impersonality, which is the god within that fiction which you adore—an unbeautiful crime in your eyes! The author is hunting for involved compensations in the heart, soul, and mind of a man about to die, and yet, are they really involved? Everything possible to heart and mind is and must be essentially *simple,* and all of the decorative subtleties and tenuous complications, which you are forever spying and decrying, are only parts of this simplicity too quick, too detailed, and too gymnastic for your approving recognition!) . . .

And so, John Musselman held this limp truce between boy and old man on his face, this discovery that different selves within human beings often fight each other not because they are different but because they struggle to be entirely distinct and to shake off the others' denied invasion. . . . The cell in which John Musselman stood was an eight-by-nine box with an oblong, barred window near the top of the rear wall and a thickly grated, barred front, with a steel door that held an opening for the passage of food and receptacles—the begrudged loophole through which life deigned to fatten one of its victims for a meanly given death. The cell had a plain cot with a white pillow and olive-drab, army blankets; a table and chair; and a screened-off toilet and washbowl in one corner of its white-washed stone and iron walls—disheartening appurtenances: the practical arrangements with which virtuous butchers advance an unnecessary and not quite sincere solicitude for the last empty moments of those whom they are about to slay? Not entirely that. . . .

The state kills men in vengeance for murder, but this open roasting or choking of flesh is only a more frankly brutal duplicate of those other killings which support our civilization—soldiers ripped and shattered in defense of shoddy, verminous "ideals" covering the clammy rivalries of money; adults and children slowly murdered in factories and mills—pardon me, if the murder is gradual, and if the victims are paid pittances for the slain freshness of bodies and minds, it becomes legal, defended, and even canonized as "honest, faithful toil"; newspapers murdering reputations and characters, with a lip-smacking paradox of banal and lurid lines and with scarcely an effort to verify the facts before rushing them into print; boys and girls, whose normal lust for each other's bodies is called unclean and dangerous, and *murdered,* or forced to gratify itself in the night-shade of public parks, in hallways, at roadhouses, in automobiles, on parlor settees—*anywhere except under the sunlight or on the meadows of that earth from which the lust sprang.* . . . No, the drab, practical contraptions within John Musselman's cell are indeed delightfully candid when compared to the inside of a church, the furnishings within a governor's or president's office, the articles in a respectable family's parlor, or the interior of a textile mill. No, the only unique hell attached to capital punishment lies in its mingling of laggard and swift elements— months in a cell but tens of years wiped out at the expiration of this time. . . .

The four months which John Musselman had spent in his crate had been generations of abortive thoughts and feelings; emotional miscarriages ad infinitum;

still-births of thought never ceasing in their imponder-
able and strangely active numbness. Ah, if the state
would only kill instantly, with an impatient virus—
but civilization at its best does not slaughter so fear-
lessly. No, it wishes to be indirect, innocently pro-
testing, judicially sifting "evidence" and waiting for
sureness, and leadenly devious in its disclaiming of
cruel motives. . . . And those who oppose capital pun-
ishment, who rise in forums to inveigh against it?—
let them repair to their supper tables and heartily eat
the flesh of murdered animals; let their women wear
the furs of cruelly trapped mink and beaver; let them
use the multitudes of articles made by moiling, sweat-
plastered serfs, whose electric chairs are stools in fac-
tories, with the current just weak enough to allow the
man or woman to walk home each night—pardon me,
ride home in body-jammed, stifling subways; let them
peer honestly into their past lives and see whether,
wittingly or unwittingly, they have never murdered the
loves, or hopes, of any other human being. Such tragic-
comic inconsistencies never bother those dramatic, de-
claiming, self-insensate people known as reformers, the
most sincere of whom are little, restricted crusaders in
a general nightmare to which they must pledge secret
allegiance. . . .

Standing in his cell, John's tall, muscular body looked
like that of a householder going to his morning bath—
brown, unheeled slippers; black cotton trousers; gray
shirt open at the throat. But one of the trouser-legs
has been slit to the knee—the respectability vanishes.

A touch of oddity, neither sinister nor harmless but inexplicable, worrisome, destroying the effect of modest négligé. . . . Life, you are a bouncing scamp. You bore a mole into the tip of the dowager's haughty beak; give a washed-out, blinking cast of eyes to the poet, so that he is mistaken for a ledger clerk; drop the shyest of dimples on the trollop's face and make her seem purer than the bundled virgin; furnish the bricklayer with a high, classical forehead; deposit the immaculate bourgeois on a bench underneath a tree and see that the refuse from birds falls on his derby hat. You have so many thousands of chuckling stunts and discrepancies to confound the preciously shaky dignities and squeezed-in prancings of human beings, and yet these men and women remain gorgeously oblivious to your disrespect. It must be so. They are the great horde of precarious, fussing, crack-mending egotists, who lack the ability to guffaw at themselves; strip to the careless lusciousness of buttocks and flanks; become, oh, so delicately amused at their own insignificance; and leave the streak of dirt on their faces for a space, instead of hastily rubbing it off. . . .

As John began his last minute of life, he gripped the edge of the table with his left hand, to steady himself. This was no fear-brought weakness but the strong desire to fall down now and have it over with, to die instantly and dispense with this senseless minute of flitting inferences, thoughts trying to crowd years of activity into a few, useless seconds, and heart-beats like the methodically clutching and slipping fingers of one dangling from a precipice, with no chance to save himself. He knew that he would die the moment he stepped from his cell door and he was glad of that, so glad—these guarding, watching people, snug in their own unthreatened skins, would not be able to gloat or blubber over any knee-bendings and squawkings on his part! Yet, if he fell to the floor and died now, it would be mistaken for the limpness of fright nevertheless, and his dead body would have to be carried to the monstrously soulless chair, and people would have a chance to pity him. No! . . .

He glanced at the window, which showed an oblong of blue sky cut into smaller, perpendicular oblongs by black bars, and skeined with the slightest fleece of tawny-white clouds. Out of nowhere the remembrance of a sky-gazing afternoon came to him—an afternoon in his earliest youth. His abnormally active brain seized this afternoon and the sequence of events which it had unleashed. His brain in a few seconds recollected the salient features within these events and sweepingly sensed the details in between. His brain had become a discoverer so swift that seconds took on the space of days to accommodate its speed. . . .

He was a boy approaching nineteen and resting underneath a tree on a field one mile west of Burnside, a suburb in the southern part of Chicago. A broad band of railroad tracks stood two hundred feet to his right and the blued silver of their flat tops gleamed in a long, straight invitation to adventure, wandering, unseen regions glamorous only because they had never

been visited. He looked up at the sky, with its huge
feathers of whitish, grayish cream clouds interfering
with the sun, but the sky was too prettily remote, too
unrelated to the big-boy gnawing he had—the con-
glomeration of rambunctious, mumbo-jumbo, check-
mated, wanting-to-burst-out loves and aches and
rumblings and most naïve of hopes. The tracks ran
out to reality, the Merciless Thing with two sides—
one chuckful of policemen's clubs; hard work, nastily
dredging strength out of the body; the goads of great
heat and coldness; girls turning him down when he'd
have split himself open for their bodies; parents always
bawling y' out when y' had some fun; worrying about
whether you'd gotten some flossie in trouble who came
across (they always lied themselves blue in the gills
'bout you being the first one); and, oh, crowds of little
things . . . the inane perversities and scratchings at-
tached to physical living, such as cutting your face
with the razor when you were in a hurry; getting end-
less spots on your suits; slipping on the dance-floor—
sometimes life seemed to be always just wa-a-aiting to
hand you a big Ha-Ha-Ha; and forgetting to button
your pants. Oho, but the other side of that Thing
which the tracks ran to—a shot of good booze, mak-
ing you feel like a grizzly bear too kind to claw; win-
ning it easy in a crap or poker game and feeling that
Chance was your faithful sweetheart 'cause she knew
all about your untried mettle; hitting the whores up
in the Red Light District; sporting good clothes that
brought you admiring looks from the girls; fighting

with a bastard and being able to smash his face; getting a hefty smile and a dollar from the old man and woman when you did something they liked, such as copping 95 in some study, watching your table manners when company came, tipping your hat to old ladies, drifting home early . . . and, oh, piles of small strokings and chin-chuckings—a girl calling you handsome (cra-ap, but still you sure ate it up); finding four bits on the street—oh, the thrill of getting something without an effort; making a good dive off the board down at the summer resort and feeling a jackknife godhood; eating a porterhouse steak with a wolfish appetite. . . .

The tracks ran out to big, unknown cities . . . Detroit . . . New Orleans . . . New York . . . Frisco . . . a fellow had told him that the flossies in Detroit were daisies and just swarming out on the corners . . . the pale cream ones, the quadroons now, down in New Orleans, they must be milk and honey. . . . Naw, it wasn't just that the niggers was better, naw, they had less shame in them and they was more honest—knew that there wasn't much real fun to living 'cept when you got it from a man, or woman, and that all the rest was flubdub, preachers' lies, covering-up so the old people wouldn't get wise to you—the old people, who'd had their fill and hated to see *you* go on having it when *they* were squelched or getting near the end . . . the old stuff. . . . "You're not going to make the mistakes I made." . . .

His experience with sex had been initiated only a year and a half before this early July afternoon now

prominent in his memory. He had been a little over
seventeen then and the first girl had been a schoolmate
of his, Mary Spielman. . . . Mary was destined to be
that curious hybrid which is neither lust nor chastity,
nor the subdued compromise of the housewife in be-
tween—an odd marriage of coldness and warmth. At
eighteen she had already had several corporeal diver-
sions. Her physical desires were practical and regu-
lated—persistently indulged in and yet incidental,
much like the taken-for-granted, unimpressed and un-
impressive appetite with which a person sits down to
his daily meals. To her it was all just feeling good and
then forgetting about it—mild expansion and deple-
tion. Such girls exist in large numbers but novelists
lie about them, or ignore them, and preachers of all
kinds minimize their numbers, shrinking from the
knowledge that sex is devoid of sentiment and wistful
fripperies and idealization in so many people. Regard
Mary Spielman, my dear preaching ones—the past
mistress of several boys, at eighteen, and not at all
frightened, nor in love, nor sentimental—in fact, not
even hardboiled, as a premature courtesan might be,
but very coolly and mildly animalish on certain nights
and very self-contained and forgetful on the mornings
following. Just a little sexual machine for a heart—
not a powerful machine but insistent nevertheless—
with intervals in which the machine became still and
Mary went to the Lutheran church of her mother, sat
at a high-school desk, made embroideries, helped her
mother with the housework, and exhibited a modesty

which was just as real as her opposite disrobings. One side of her simply continually forgot what the other side was doing. But the darling preachers are intruding again—these Mary Spielmans are either subnormal or ferociously oversexed, abnormal. "Normal people are more complicated, more repressed, more in the grip of conscience and conflicts." Yes? A horse in harness may be more subtle than a tiger, or an indulging rabbit, but the evidence would seem to be to the contrary. Normal people are dull, one-colored, and intent upon using every device that can change an essential endurance-feat to a virtuous and denied martyrdom, and their seeming complications, interplays of conscience, warfares between suppressions and secret nibblings, are little more than the grunts, foot-stampings, shiftings, and tossings of animals tied to the old cart of respectability but resting, or excursioning, a little at night, when the reins and bits become much looser, more unseen. It is not entirely a matter of flesh under bondage. The minds and souls of indubitably normal people are just strong enough to vitiate the animal fear of these men and women and make them tame, self-questioning, vapidly suspended between outburst and death. When the person revolts, his normality dies and his mind and soul bring distinguished, plausible, and weightless rescues to the previously trapped solidity of his desires—then clergymen run off with choir-leaders; housewives desert husbands and children for a first real romance with some dreamy-eyed shoe clerk, however tawdrily this romance may end; society-débutantes throw off the hated lie of culture and hook up with day-laborers; doctors maintain concealed mistresses, while fulminating at the "immorality" of other men; middle-aged, foreign mothers in the slums suddenly kill their recreant husbands; prizefighters read Shakespeare and Thornton Wilder—an inappropriate but effective combination—and become bored with slugging; college girls rob banks, or dress in men's clothes and ride in freight cars . . . a small percentage of the whole, perhaps, but never-ending, and not nearly as limited as apologists assert.

Mary Spielman belonged to another class, neither normal nor abnormal, and certainly not a cretin, but just a very moderate, giggling, conscienceless animal, mating and then going back to an untroubled dreamlessness, with the precision, the inevitability, and the fearlessness of a clawless and toothless dog, or cat. Eventually she was to marry, and be faithless to her husband once or twice a year during the first ten and then faithful to him after that simply because of a tremendous lessening in physical desires, and she was to assume a dutiful air toward him because it salvaged her comforts and her liaisons of one night every six months or so, and feel toward him an "Oh-he's-all-right-and-he-means-well" reaction, and raise a family without expecting her sons and daughters to be different from what she had been, but lecturing and watching them just the same because this was the Great Generally Accepted Lie of Life—a lie so cogent

and volubly self-denying that it took on all the guises
and protestations of Truth! . . .

As John sat underneath the tree and alternately
stared at the hard shooting-out of the tracks and the
soft curving-out of the oblivious sky, he remembered
parts of his first introduction to sex in Mary's house.
He had strolled with her after school hours to ice-cream
parlors, and once to a two-reel Wild West Movie—
motion pictures were then in their crude infancy—
but he had never before been alone with her. He looked
upon her as a jolly, not bright or stupid, regular girl,
who was neither pretty nor homely—just indeterminate
and fairly pleasing because she rattled off the small-
talk of his life, looked up to him as an athlete—he
was on the basketball and baseball teams—and was
willing to kiss him good-by at the house door. He had
heard whispers among the boys that she was among
the few "easy" girls at their school but he knew that
they often liked to make themselves feel big—by claim-
ing to have had this girl and that, and he couldn't rely
upon such testimony. Still, when they boasted, it made
him feel ashamed of never having had a girl—gee
whiz, he was getting to be a man now, and all the semi-
mysterious, delicious, luscious, squirming pleasure of
girls was waiting for his cruel, triumphant enjoyment
. . . he knew what it was all about—oh, boy, but didn't
he!—and he just had to vindicate the hairs on his
chest and be able to hold his head up with an I'm-
getting-mine pride and escape from fidgetings and
nasty-nice but useless dreams every night, and ye-e-es,

maybe fall head-over-toes in love with some curly-haired, shiny-eyed, curvy, wonderful pippin of a girl and meet her on the sly and trade warm notes with her and go straight to heaven in her arms, while they both swore to stick together forever. Oh, hell, it wouldn't last, of course, but there was always others just as marvelous, sure there was. . . . Gee, a man could roam 'round and take his pick, like a king, 'less he was a batter-faced runt, or a Simple Simon, and then afterwards he could marry a decent, pretty girl—*nobody else's leavings* but a virgin just bursting-sweet and aching to find out—and settle down and have a bunch of kids to be proud of.

But what's this?—spurts of involuntary pessimism from some nook as yet uncharted within his heart, shaking the tum-dee-dee optimism just a little. His ma, now, she must have been a snippy humdinger when she was young—those photos in the album proved she'd been prettier than any girl he knew—but *now* . . . quarreling with his pa sometimes and hollering she wished she had never married him, and great big wrinkles on her face with her only forty-four—poor ma, she'd worked and worried damn hard in her time! And his pa, cussing over house-painting jobs, over the rent, over John himself, and his brother, Julius, and Elsa, his sister, and over the way ma spent money— the only time pa never cussed was on Saturday night before he went down to Sloan's saloon for a lot of beer and auction-pinochle. Hell, men got a few years of pleasure out of life, right at the start, and then they got their noses plastered 'gainst that grindstone and everything petered out to a lot of work and a little drinking and cards. Well, sure, 'cause they was foolish enough to get married right away 'stead of staying free and independent. Christ, a man would always have to sweat his insides out working but if he wasn't tied down to a wife and kids he could quit his job and go to another city, or save up a roll and then spread it for a sweet month or two of whoring and likkering, or go 'round with good girls every night and get some of them, if he was a crackerjack spieler. He, John, would never marry unless he had a pile of dough and didn't have to quit all the fun and hell-splitting of living. Sti-i-ill, suppose he met a baby-mine so all-fired beautiful and so perfect a fit for his ways of doing things that he just couldn't live without her, and she wouldn't give herself up 'less he married her? . . .

The old collision between two brands of sensuality, one unwittingly cruel, and stripped, and gluttonous, and the other seeking sentimentally to deny its own identity, recoiling from its own monotonous coarseness, bearing the little canker of self-disgust which philosophers cannot explain because it invades even their own systems of explanation, and ruled by the Great Jekyll and Hyde Fundamental of so many human hearts—selfishness posing as unselfishness because it fears to cheapen and degrade the value of those objects which it craves most of all. Why? The difference between man and animal lurks behind this never quite answerable question—the difference between direct action and cunning rationalizing; between rending hunger and hunger ashamed of its teeth; between sweating, honest lunges and equally vicious attacks staged behind pratings of honor, decency, vigilant affection. . . .

John dismissed this conflict with the credulous, nerves-supreme, hard laugh of youth—rake in your flossies while you could and if you did marry one of them, that didn't mean that you couldn't keep on having a good time if you insisted on being the boss and if you kept from having kids for a long while. Didn't see how you could keep from it, but there must be a way. His knowledge made him feel like a finished man of the world—knew all the tricks, he did. High time he put them to some use and showed the other fellows what an up-to-date kingpin he was. 'Course, he could go down to the Red Light District but that would be an affront to his pride—as though he was so stuck-to-the-wall and ungifted that he had to pay a girl to make out that she liked him. No, he'd win his first girl by making her really fall for his build and the turn of his style, and she'd be just mad about his face and the chest he had, and then he'd be actually launched on his way, with something that he could boast of to himself. . . .

Let's see, who were the most possible ones among the girls he knew? Mabel Flannagan? Aw, she had a nose like a parrot's beak and she was so nervous she went into fits of giggles whenever he touched her— he'd rather tag after a six-year-old! Helen Brewster?

Well, yes and no. She was willing to kiss a hundred times but she was the 'fraidy-cat kind and one night, when his hands had become restless at a party, she had whispered afterwards: "Jo-ohnnie, does this mean we're going to marry each other, huh?" She'd probably run to her mother the next day, if he really came close to her, and then he *would* be in a peck of trouble. Amy Schoenberg? Amy was a good sport, all right, but those sheeny girls were hard to get—their old men and women watched them like sixty and always hung 'round the room when a boy called, and came in at ten o'clock and politely put him out. Picnics and walks out in the field were always a way out but it was winter now—nothing stirring. . . .

Well, how about Mary Spielman? She wasn't a holy wonder in her looks but she wasn't bad, either, with her long, curly, brown hair, and her loose lips always smiling a little, and her fat body with its cream-brown skin. Her father was dead and she had no brothers and only one sister, who was married and lived on the North Side, and her mother often went out at night— belonged to some kind of club for helping poor people. The lay of the land couldn't have been better, but he didn't know whether he stood a tinker's chance with Mary, 'spite of what the boys said about her. She'd let him kiss her, sure, but whenever he'd tried anything else, when they stood at her door and she was telling him good night, she had cut him short with an abruptness that had been quite different from the tactics of other girls, with their "Oh, don't, don't, please do-on't"

while they never made a move to take your hands
away, or the weak fights they put up that showed they
was *half* willing anyway, or the way in which they let
him until he got real off, and then jumped up and
pitched into him, as though they hadn't known what
he was up to . . . humph, the cheap, little flirts. He
remembered what Mary had said one night just after
breaking away from him. "Johnny, don't be silly in a
place like this—I don't want it this way." Had she
meant that she didn't want him to take her, or that a
doorway wasn't the right place for it? She was a deep
one sometimes—made remarks that might be yes or
no—but that made it a nicer gamble. Who the heck
wanted a girl that *didn't* twist around or get a boy out
of breath before he bagged her? Otherwise, if it was
so darn easy, a boy figgered out that it must have been
just as easy for other fellows and this didn't make his
victory amount to much unless he knew the girl had
a real, crazy, hope-to-die love for him and wouldn't
go out with a single other boy. . . . Yes, he'd make his
first, do-or-die try in Mary's direction.

His callow overtures began one afternoon, as Mary
and he were walking out of the barracklike, black-
slate-topped, red brick and gray stone high school,
whose appearance somehow exuded the very essence
of public-school education, which is so often conform-
ity and information saying nay to initiative. He felt
his way tentatively, almost dizzily, beneath the gruff
casualness which he tried to assume.

"Aw, say, Mary, lemme come up to your house to-night, will you?"

"What for?"

"What fo-or? Say, if you don't like me I'll make myself scarce right now. It don't matter a whoop to me."

She looked at him with sprightly, oh-you-liar appraisement.

"Now, Johnny, you know I didn't mean tha-at."

Some silence.

"We-ell, what about to-night, then?"

"We-e-ell."

"Two wells make a river and you in the middle!"

They snickered at this.

"Lissen, Johnny, ma won't be home till 'leven to-night—she goes to the Children's Aid League Tuesdays and Fridays."

"What about it?"

"Course she wouldn't let me see you, not if she knew you was coming up. It's not right for girls to be alone with boys (a giggle), leastways ma says it's not."

"Aw, it's not right to bre-e-eathe if you lissen to your old man 'r your old woman. They make me sick."

"Now, Johnny, you mustn't talk that way 'r I'll begin to think you're a ba-ad boy."

"Well, I can't stop you from thinking, can I?"

They both grinned at each other.

"I'll be up at eight to-night—your ma'll be out by that time, won't she?"

"Sure she will, but *I* didn't say you could, Mister Johnny. Guess I've got *something* to say about it."

"All right, then; maybe I'll stop talking to you and we'll just leave each other alone. I've never chased after a girl yet after she's made it good 'n' plain that she don't want to be with me. . . . So long, Mary."

He began to walk away—not as aggrieved as he seemed to be but sulkily scratched and sincere nevertheless. She had been fiddling with him for three reasons—she wanted to see how he would take it; she had a girlish desire to be gorgeously courted while she hemmed and hawed to keep it going; and also, though she had occasionally received boys at her home during her mother's absences, she was always "on pins 'n' needles 'bout it"—not afraid of being caught, or tongue-whipped, but fearing that detection might end the tingly, just-nice-enough, sigh-dipped departures from the more orderly and dressed-up observances of her life. Now, when she saw that he was striding off in earnest, she respected his huffy, sassy, big-boy attitude—he was strong, and he had black eyes that were bossy without being mean, and he was on all the teams and looked-up-to as one of the school's leaders in everything except his studies—he wasn't much in the latter but who cared about that? Studies were things that had to be endured and wriggled through and those who excelled in them were most always sissies, or mopes, or teachers' pets.

She hastened after him and grabbed his arm.

"Gee, look what I'm doing now—running after you. Gee, that ought to make you even with me now."

He stopped, smacking his lips over this honied comedown but trying to look as if he had expected it.

"Aw, who wants to get even with you. You know I like you, Mary, 'cause if I didn't I wouldn't have let you tease me one minute, not me."

"Oh, sure I do, Johnny. Lissen, you can come up to my house 'bout eight to-night, if you still want to, but you've got to ring the bell three times, see? It'll be a signal, see, 'cause if ma doesn't go out then I'll run to the door and make out, we-e-ell, make out you came to bring me something I lost at school. That's it."

"Yep, that'll be slick," he answered, feeling already like a monumental roué, who had been idling before his task merely because he hadn't wanted to become sated and gorged too soon. (Oh, happiness is the elixir with which human molecules rise to a gargantuan rape of reality!)

More words between John and Mary—the troglodyte plainness of bodies moving toward each other beneath a juvenile fussiness tendered by civilized environment. Put Mary and John in a lily-bordered, tall-treed dell on the farthest edge of the world and let them crush the flowers beneath the unfathomable simplicity of their lust, you people who are forever pouncing upon the flesh-desires of youths and maidens and pounding them apart with your furious envies and impotencies, your scanty imaginations stuffed up with indignation, your grubbing annoyance at those who dream a little of "flying" before you pull them down. Sentimental bitterness? No, just a tear glistening for a second on the unhoping brightness of thought. Your own furies and disdains are real, but mine are only wounds talking themselves to sleep. . . .

John sat in the parlor of Mary's house and felt ridiculous, and lachrymose, and determined, and whenever one of the three bumped against the other within him, he made another remark in his quest for ease. He had been alone with plenty of girls but never with such an absolute resolve to bring matters to a conclusion. It had been just fooling around before—scarcely hoping that he could get them and making himself be contented with kisses and hugs, but now he was a ma-an out for the first conquest that would clinch his adulthood, and the momentousness of it to him made him rattled, and taciturn. He sat with Mary on the black horsehair sofa and they looked at each other—*she* was fully at ease, tittering, and but mildly aroused. Would he or wouldn't he? She didn't care much—this not-knowing at the start and this playing around with a boy was really the best part of it because then she felt so high-handed, so beautifully precious and sought-after, so zestfully balanced between yes and no, although she knew which it would be—yes, if she liked the boy's face and manners, and no, if she didn't—but still it was nicer to make-believe that she wasn't going to decide until he tried and begged again and again. After these preliminaries it was good, ye-es, but nothing so wonderful—she lost her queenliness

then and felt just a little hurt, abased, over-accommo-
dating: just a little, beneath the whipped pleasure. . . .

As the minutes passed, John became less rattled—
the multi-sided, posing, rosy cheekiness of youth came
to his rescue with its aw-who-the-hell-cares accompani-
ments. Kid her along for a while and show her he
wasn't so darn anxious. If it wasn't her on this night
it would be another girl on a different evening. He
tapped his fingers on a glass dome that shielded wax-
flowers and stood on a wobbly, three-legged taboret
beside the low sofa—tapped the beat of a bugle-call
he'd heard at the last Fourth of July parade. . . .
Young girls take warning, young girls take wa-arning.
. . . So-oldier-lads know how, but they'll leave in the
mo-orning. . . . He'd heard a soldier bawling that in
a corner saloon once.

"Think you'll pass the exams?"

"Gosh, I hope so," she answered. "I only got
seventy-five in Ancient His' last month but that fussy
Missus Peters sits in the rear and just watches all the
time to see if we've got the book in our laps."

"She gives me a headache."

"Me, too."

"I only got sixty in Geom' last time and that growly
one, Parker, he bawled me out right in front of the
whole bunch. He said: 'You may be a corker on the
ball team, Musselman,' he said, 'but you're just a plain
dunce when you get in front of that blackboard.' Gee,
I felt so-ore, I can tell you."

"I had him in Alg' when I was a freshie, and sa-ay,

I still don't know how I ever got through. I put a big bunch of flowers in the vase on his desk one morning and he looked like he was tickled pink about it. Guess that was it."

"You girls would have a holy cinch all right, if they was all men teachers."

She giggled and he lit a cigarette which he had stolen from his elder brother—he "wasn't allowed" to smoke on the ground that it would stunt his growth though his family knew that he smoked on the sly. Their school small-talk slowly petered out and was replaced by more intimate gossipings.

"Say, did you know Bill Sulzer was Rose Finley's beau?" she asked.

"Aw you're foolish—she's sweet on Carl Jenowitch, that big bohunk slob, she is."

"She *was,* you mean. She had a big tiff with him 'cause she asked him to tie her shoelace the other day and he says: 'You can bend down yourself, can't you?', he says. Well, that got her awf'lly sore, and I don't blame her either."

"Well, gee whiz, a boy looks silly kneeling right down in front of a girl. I'll bet you it was right in the hallway too, wasn't it?"

"Ye-eh, right in front of Room Ten."

"Hu-uh, d'you suppose he wanted everybody to get a laugh on him?"

"I . . . don't . . . care . . . about . . . that. A boy ought to be polite, specially if he's gone on a girl."

"Well, catch *me* doing anything like that! You girls 'r' always wanting a boy to wait on you."

Silence. Mary a little peeved but not really minding: John feeling exquisitely self-assertive.

"You didn't go to Mabel's party last week, did you?"

"Naw, I had to stay home 'cause ma was sick and all the rest of the folks was out. I get the worst of it all the time. D'you hear what was doing at the party?"

"Di-id I-i? Sa-ay, the way Mabel spooned with George Franzine was simply terrible. Her ma caught them out in the ba-ack-ya-ard, of a-all the pla-aces, and I'll bet Mabe got it good 'n' heavy."

"What was they pulling out there? Gee, it must have been at least ten above that night."

"Mabel, she said they just went out to look at the mo-o-on—that's a good one, isn't it?"

"Ye-eh, a good piece of mu-ush, that's what."

"Why, Johnny, don't you ever get mushy?"

"Oh, I guess so, but I don't need no moon to back *me* up."

She laughed hesitantly.

"Well, you certainly act like you needed it," she answered.

The hint was clear and he slid over to her side, put an arm around her waist, and kissed her. She leaned back on the sofa and smiled at him—an aren't-you-bold?, leading-on, gauzily expectant and yet just a bit careful smile. The next half hour passed as he kissed and hugged her, while she put on just that usual fig-

ment of struggling and withdrawal which she felt to be
her prerogative, even when she had made up her mind
to drop it before the end—the old sex-wriggle, sex-
defense, that never quite perishes. (I have seen soul-
corrugated prostitutes shrink from a man for a
moment, when he had become too roughly precipitate,
and then return to their passive acceptance, as though
a little firecracker of delicateness had fizzed up and
died.) . . .

The simple hunger's on you now, John—so dark, so
heavy with all the vibrant, near-poisonous, musty,
heady mystery of earth in a dream of escape from all
the grayness, all the brownness, all the shackled green-
ness of its outward forms. Dream-scream of escape
. . . maligned by moralists; worshiped by pagans;
turned to a half-bound, conscious vassal by apostles
of moderation; disowned in public and privately wel-
comed by compromisers—the earth will never be free
until you are brought forth into the real sunlight on
any field, or street, and accepted as openly, naturally,
and casually as the process of breathing, which means
. . . that the earth will never be free. . .

John tried to push her shoulders back on the sofa
and she stopped him. He was almost surly now—he
could have pummeled her, commanded her with pro-
fanities, for the fire in him had consumed all of the
specious refinements and sparings plastered on him by
his "bringing-up," but he was also just enough scared
to be an inch removed from unthinking frenzy—her
mother might always walk in; he might get into trouble

afterwards; Mary might yell and attract the neigh-
bors' attention. . . . Adolescent goblins, products of
inexperience. Even the craziness in his veins had barely
to hold itself in leash.

"Are you . . . going to . . . let me?" he asked, the
words popping in between his hard breathings.

She gave him a chiding grin and stretched her arms
with the utmost of placidity.

"Oh, I suppose I'll have to," she said. "It's
na-au-ughty, but . . . I don't ca-are. It's nice, too."

This sheer, relaxed, ungilded carelessness—so far
removed from all of his previous ideas on how a girl
would act in such a crisis—took him aback and made
the impending happening seem weaker, more cut-and-
dried, no longer a preciousness to be fought for, and
deprived of all glamorous flatterings, recoilings, sweetly,
oh so sweetly enfevered words before the girl gave up
her last shred of coyness and you both swore that
you'd stay together until death parted you, even if
you didn't mean it. Gosh, but this was *some* come-
down—so darn plain, and easy, and oh, kind of almost-
ugly.

"Gee, doesn't it mean a whole lot to you?" he asked,
as he caressed her with an engine-like lack of spirit.
"Ge-ee, Mary, you're cool's a cucumber 'bout it."

"Johnny, you're such a funny boy," she answered.
"Su-uch a fu-u-unny—"

"No, but doesn't it?"

"Oh, it's just having a good time f'r a while—what
else *could* it be? I don't lo-ove you, course not, but

I do like you heaps, 'n' heaps, 'n' we-ell, I can't see why we've got to waste so much ti-ime. I *told* you I would, didn't I?"

She pulled at his arm and the clangings and sirens took undisputed hold of his breast. Never mind whether it *was* a come-down, with no polish and no turtle-dove words to it. He'd start to *live* from this moment on: he'd be a man now, through and through —a big, heartless, hairy, girl-grabbing man . . .

John's first experience with Mary—and the occasional sneaking reiterations that followed it—was to exert a profound though unobtrusive influence on the remainder of his sexual life. He was by nature a sentimentalist in spite of all the boyish snarls, champings, and verbal befoulings, which spring from unsheltered environments where most of the boys, as a matter of physical pride, try to emulate the few toughest and most cantankerous ones among them. When a sentimentalist's budding sighs for perfumes, dissimulations, and kneeling trepidations are immediately kicked by dénouement and practicality, he takes on a defense-mechanism; he tucks away his contused softness and sets out to make himself a hard, roistering, unbending creature, partly to avenge the first blow and partly to protect himself against future ones. As the months passed and Mary receded out of his life— she had been a mere convenience, and with the advent of sexual surety he had dropped her for a prettier girl —he steeled himself to look upon sex as a stereotyped, tricking, flesh-rewarding business—business-deals in which you got the better of the girl, or lost out, with a fair degree of composure. All sentiments were relegated to mouthings that were only part of your technique, and though you came near to feeling them in earnest, if the girl was a stunning lulu and you got along remarkably well with each other, this relenting had to be crushed, forgotten. The atmosphere of boy-chums prattling about new catches and gathering to measure up this girl and that was too fetching to allow you to fall heavy for one girl and maybe let her make a fool out of you. . . . Mary had certainly opened his eyes—sex was just a free-for-all where the coolest people won out, or weren't all broken up if they didn't, while the others got kicked in the pants 'less they was lucky enough to find the one person in thousands who really fitted into them and thought they was cock of the walk.

When he had gone to the Red Light District of Chicago and consorted with strumpets there, he had liked them far more than the decent, near-decent, and respectably chattering girls of his neighborhood and nearby regions, even those among the girls who had capitulated later. The prostitutes were straight-from-the-shoulder, kidding-for-business, unhampered women —they knew it was all a physical thing and they didn't blubber, and wince, and babble around it. They gave him no fake-struggles and no requests for life-long affection. Most of them were cold, and scheming, and liars down to the bone, sure, but he'd caught de-cent girls in just as many lies, come to think of it, and if you acted brassy and scoffing to the bad girls they stopped trying to work you and treated you with a little squareness. And some few among them were big-hearted, palish peaches—look at that Polish one, Anna Koscienski, the one he'd picked up in Colosimo's joint, who could have frisked him for his roll easy, since he'd been stewed to the gills, but who had brought him to with spirits of ammonia and told him to take better care of his poke. Thirty bucks saved up from subbing for Pete Daley behind the bar at Sloan's saloon—boy, what a close shave that had been! . . . Aw heck, the best skirts were the ones you had no reason to trust at all and the worst ones often bobbed up right in your own crowd—like Martha Stacey, who'd gotten money from three boys 'cause she told each boy she was caught and he was the father. She'd have roped *him* in too, if he hadn't been wised up about it. Course, any fellow got scairy when he saw those bars waiting to coop him in. . . .

He sprawled out under the tree, with the back of his head cupped between his flung-back forearms, and stared up at the Indian-feather clouds scarcely moving against the inhuman, washed-out blue of the sky. That gray cloud underneath the higher ones looked like a man with whiskers, or he'd be jugged. Aw hell, only mollies got dreamy-eyed and made up things like that. But the cloud *was* a dead ringer for a man's face just the same—look at that outline of a nose and chin— and O-oh we-ell, it was all right to be a molly and see queer things and love to pick bunches of wild flowers and get so damn soft inside you couldn't recognize yourself, if you didn't show this weaker side to any one—the boys in particular: they'd swat you in a minute—and kept it from bouncing up all the time lest it make you an out-and-out si-ill'. He wouldn't be surprised if most men had just a little girly, dreamy, snivelly stuff in them—with the exception of downright thugs and plug-uglies—but they kept it to themselves. Hadn't he caught even his pa taking a pressed, dry flower from a book at the house and talking to himself as he held it in his palm and looked at it? Pa had cussed him out for snooping around and then begged him not to tell ma about it. Some old girl had once given the flower to pa, he'd bet a dollar on it! . . .

Funny, sometimes men didn't marry the woman they loved most, and afterwards, every now and then they felt sorry about it. This marrying-business was a puzzler to him—they all quarreled, and worked harder and harder to pay the bills, and looked kinda longing at women who was single—he'd seen married men standing on the corner near Sloan's and eying up the girls that passed—and often had trouble with their kids, but they claimed to like it, or else they said every man had to go through it anyway. Deep stuff, too deep for him. He'd probably marry some day, since most men did, but he wasn't exactly happy at the prospect. Ye-e-ess, he'd finally go plumb dippy over a girl who wouldn't give in 'less he married her, or else some skirt would smash him up for fair and

he'd get sore and through with all of it, and marry
the best one that came along, just to escape from get-
ting another knock. Jimminy-whillikins, couldn't he
think of something pleasant for a change?

Here he was, just graduated from High and starting
out to make his way in the world, and everything was
up to him—if he had grit, and used his head, and didn't
let people get the better of him, he might rise to the
top of the heap and have money and a fine wife, or
women galore, and a horseless-carriage, and a mansion
for a home . . . and . . . and . . . what was lack-
ing, why wasn't he quite satisfied with this big array,
what was wrong? Money, fine clothes, servants—he
kept repeating them in a tom-tom that struck against
an opposition, dim, never guessed before, but indis-
soluble. He wanted to be different from other people
—oh, beginning ache of originality, dropped into a few
breasts to be reviled, or misunderstood by millions of
others: dropped by a perverse force to which the
thyroid-glands and hereditary-influences extracted by
science are the veriest of playthings—to go them one
better, but how? He didn't like to study—his mind al-
ways buzzed and shrank from the compilations of
dry facts and figures, and the effort required to absorb
them—and he wasn't fond of manual labor, with its
sweats, and dullness, and orders, though he could force
himself to do it because there was no other way of
earning money and he didn't want to be a bum, de-
spised and laughed at by other men—and working in
an office would crate him up and make him moil with

endless rows of figures, which he hated—his math'
teachers had passed him out of sheer charity . . . so
what was left?

He turned and looked again at the bands of railroad-
tracks two hundred feet to his right—they made his
feet itch and brought a dare-devilish, painful motion
to his heart. Detroit . . . Buffalo . . . Los Angeles
. . . new scenes and faces, teeming with realizations
of hope based on nothing but the sightless, uncut in-
flammations of youth . . . and the lust for wander-
ing, to flee from the immediate monotony of reality
only to remain within a larger monotone and yet to
nullify this larger one's effect with a constant exchange
of exteriors and all their little differences—narrow
streets, sloe-eyed, palely clouded faces, balconied
doll's houses in the Creole Quarter of New Orleans;
high, Spanish garden walls and elaborately low roofs,
darkly lazy Mexican faces, the Buckhorn Saloon with
hundreds of antlers, and prongs, and deer-heads stud-
ding its walls, in San Antonio; red-brick and white
woodwork, Colonial Houses huddled on the steep rises
of Beacon Hill in Boston, and the Boston Commons
with its statues, pools, flowers, and lawns glossier and
more fastidiously soulless than any other American
public-park. . . .

Should he become a 'bo and just knock around for
a year or two? Gee, he had a long time to live and he
could pick up a lot of experience that way. Bill Schol-
linger had bummed his way clear to Frisco and back
again twice and Bill had told him that a man never

knew how to take care of himself till he was slammed around and felt his belly dropping out from no food, 'cause if he had it easy all the time then he wasn't in trim when a pinch came. Something in that, but Christ, it couldn't be the only way to rake in wiseness and it sure was a lousy graft, with the railroad dicks laying for you all the time and with one slip in your hold on the baggage-car blinds meaning that you got the wheels underneath. Still, all of that was taking a *man's chance*—jamming your cap down over your eyes and clamping your teeth together and showing that you could get by on your own in spite of every danger. Then again, it wasn't bad to loll by the tracks and think of all the stiffs who were pounding their insides out working for little or nothing . . . that sprawling, unambitious, futilely dreaming child of imagination, which men call laziness, took his heart solidly for a time and would not move, saw nothing in physical motion but an obnoxious, stretched-out sameness, where perspiring strivings of legs and arms contended vainly against the eventual laziness of the grave, and where thoughts cared only for slow absorption, contemplation. . . .

The lure died down within him—naw, he wouldn't be getting anything out of life then—just thrown about, and looking on from the outside, and not mixed up in the hot, racing, bullying contest of people and things, and forced to mooch for nickels and dimes and have fools look down on him. The different dream of application, where imagination tries to prove itself

more real than the seemingly weightier stagnancies
and cancelations which oppose it, bubbled and swished
in his veins—an equally futile dream, less connected
with the watching stillness of any man's soul, but one
that challenges the brutality of time and the leer of a
universe with a truly diverting desperation. . . .

What should he do during the summer months, just
marking time till the fall? How about getting on a
semi-pro ball team? No, he wasn't good enough—a
dandy fielder but no batting eye: couldn't hit a curve
ball to save his life. He'd made some hits on the school
team, of course, but the pitchers he'd faced then had
been pie compared to what he'd have to bat against in
the semis with some of the pitchers almost ripe for
big-league twirling. Besides, he wasn't crazy about
baseball. Couldn't keep his mind on the ball and
started to think of a hundred other things. The strain
and blare of competition, with the delighted shrieks
of boys and girls to urge on his vanity, had somehow
failed to penetrate to his blood. There wasn't any
bigness, or meaning, to grabbing the apple and wing-
ing it to a baseman's mit, except that it showed that
he had muscle and a quick arm, but so did thousands
of other boys. There was nothing different attached
to it, nothing that would make people point him out
as the Only One, nothing that was splendid, and up
in the air, and far-reaching. Gosh, he didn't know how
he wanted to be different—he just knew that it was
there, and wondered if he'd keep on wishing all his
life while tinkering with this iob and that and getting

nowhere. Well, nothing immediate could be done about it and the gay, warmly scampering, scented, shouting su-ummer was calling to him. Bo-oy, if he could only go to South Haven, Michigan, and flip his new breast-stroke in the friendly pull of the water, and make the girls' eyes pop out with his butterfly-dive, and half bury himself in the sand and feel pleasantly lashed and limbered-up and void of everything except thoughts of who'd be the next girl and what a whopping meal was waiting for him. . . .

A-ah he-e-ell, the family expected him to work steadily this summer—bus' slack with pa (his father was a house-painter, who contracted for jobs and then hired men to help him) and Julius working half time now (his older brother, who toiled as a mechanic in the Illinois Central roundhouse in Burnside) and Elsa (his sixteen-year-old sister) just getting over a broken arm sustained from a tumble off the wood pile in the back yard—he had chased her there because she had poured salt in his coffee and he'd been blamed for the accident, *of course*—and ma with her off'n-on sickness that nobody could explain—one doc' called it lumbago and the other said it was neuritis. . . . What was it—this endless fight against ills, and bills, and lay-offs, and raps? Life was a crazy, unfair, skin-flintish dumb-ox, flabbergasting and yet damn attractive thing (these precise adjectives did not emerge in his mind, but a wordless approach to them fought in his head). This luck-stuff now—the Sullivans next door got by like a breeze . . . healthy pigs; never a

scratch or a bump; and the old man raking in his
regular sixty a week as a master-plumber (a munif-
icent stipend at that time). His uncle Fritz too—
bought a lot on the North Side twenty years ago and
tried to sell again and again but nobody would take it,
and now a big hotel bought it for fifty thousand. This
Luck grabbed people like they was cards in a deck
and he was shuffling them and dealing them out and
not caring which ones was going to win and which
wasn't. Maybe Luck himself didn't know—just mixed
up the cards and let it happen. . . .

Gee, queer things were bobbing up in his head to-
day—must be 'cause he had time to think now. Usu-
ally he was studying just enough to squeeze by, or
chopping wood and fixing things 'round the house, or
sliding out beer and booze at Sloan's in the afternoon
and listening to the dirty jokes and drinking a little
on the sly when Sloan wasn't watching. All except at
night, when he was with some girl, or chaffing with a
bunch of them on the corner of Ninety-third Street
and Cottage Grove Avenue in front of Barry's Pool
Room. No chance to think with the flossies around,
Christ no, and besides, they didn't want you to thi-i-ink
—if you had ever made a deep remark to *them,* they
would have laughed their heads off and called you
weak in the dome. They wanted you to talk about
what was going on in the crowds you all knew, and
hand the low-down on what boys and girls were travel-
ing with each other, and scuffle with them without
going too far, and treat them to an ice-cream soda, and

tell them you'd like to be their one and only beau when both of you knew it was bean porridge, and give you sugar-candy when they didn't like you so much but wanted you to show them a good time, and o-oh ye-e-es, sometimes they'd get serious and talk about marrying and babies, and how girls got rid of kids, and how their folks was always on top of them for every little thing, but even then it never lasted long and most of it was common as mud. . . .

We-ell, all of this wasn't deciding what he was going to do this summer—nothing heavy but just something to kill time and make a little money before September. Sloan's was too hot in the summer and when there was a rush on the bar you didn't even have time to draw a beer for yourself and cool off. Something out in the air would be better. Ice-toting, grocery-delivering, house-painting—he could swing a neat brush when he had to—they were all sweaty grinds. Say, how about a peanut or pop-corn job at the White Sox Ball Park? They paid you two bucks a game and gave you a percentage on all the bags you sold over three hundred for each game, and you could watch the playing, especially in the last two innings when nobody bought much. Of course, it was a cheap, doggish job for any one with the least brains, and the family would ask him why he didn't put some axle grease in his elbows—the harder you worked the more they bowed down to you, no matter how little you earned!—but he'd have plenty of time in the future for tough jobs, if that was all he was going to amount

to, and he just wanted to drift through the hot months
by hook or crook and then make a beauty of a splurge
in the fall—work his way through the University of
Chicago or practice up on his clog-dancing and get a
chance on the stage—his family had laughed at the
ten-dollar prize he'd won on Amateurs' Night at "The
Star And Garter" a half year ago but just the same
the boss there had told him he was a comer, or . . .
or . . . the multitudinous, snatching-at-air, gymnas-
tic, scintillating plans and aggrandizements of youth
seethed in all of the unmarked dreaminess of his heart.
. . . A boy held down, blinkered, and boxed-up by
the first years of his environment and yet holding that
superhumanly preserved, inexplicable spark which dif-
ferentiates the "sport" from the more unified members
of any species.

He raised himself to an upright position underneath
the tree and plucked at a brown-eyed susan, snipping
off the tips of the petals with a negligent, half-absent-
minded whim of destruction—the tyranny with which
human beings' power of motion congratulates itself
at the expense of inanimate objects and life (I have
seen a clergyman tear a dandelion to pieces while read-
ing a bible on the grass of a public park). Should he
go home now?—his Ingersoll watch said it was nearly
four-thirty . . . aw, no, it was good to laze around
here and think things over and find a kind of hearty,
uncanny, lenient peace in the grass, weeds, and flowers,
and feel set apart from all the noises and demanding
bodies and stiffness attached to buildings and streets.

These were his feelings translated into words a little
clearer and more compact than the ones which slid
and blundered within him.

Far off on the edge of the field, where a barbed-
wire fence separated it from a swampy patch spiked
with brown and green cat-o'-nine-tails, he saw a girl,
or woman, stooping sometimes to pick the susans,
buttercups, wild-roses, and tailor-ribbons—throngs
of flowers ruffled by the breeze to impromptu, scampish
songs, with the different colors and their shades trans-
ferring notes of sound—pale blue was C sharp; pink
was D; red was G; yellow was B flat; green was A
minor. John did not detect the songs but he thought
that the flowers were fine 'n' elegant—helpless,
smoothly glowing things, like good girls who'd never
been touched, or rather, like such girls were when
they stood, or sat still, and just turned you upside-
down with their loveliness, 'cause when they began to
talk they came down to earth again and made babyish
digs, and newsy tattly remarks, and uttered tons of
flubdub.

He peered out at the distant figure—seemed to be a
slender girl but might be a granny for all he knew.
She was wearing a dark blue dress that stopped be-
tween the ankles and knees, and her dark hair came
down in broad coils against the nape of her neck.
Should he sort of ramble over and make up to her if
she turned out to be young and not impossible-looking?
Naw, he liked this feeling of being alone and letting
everything go hang for a while. Christ, no use in go-

ing after them like a machine—had to forget them
sometimes. As he sat, idly watching her and more
interested than his desire for disdainful self-sufficiency
cared to admit, he heard the sound of barking and saw
a mongrel leaping in a direct line toward the flower-
picker. Probably her dog, or one running up to make
friends with her, but no . . . it was jumping straight
at her now and tearing at her dress, while she backed
away and seemed to be bewildered as she still hung
on to her big bunch of posies. Holy smoke, it must be
a mad dog attacking her. He jumped to his feet and
as he did, she dropped her flowers and began to run
down the field, with the dog springing after her. He
began to hurry toward her and then abruptly checked
himself—might not be able to get the brute with his
bare hands. He looked desperately around him and
then picked up a large rock and hastened forward
again. The girl was only twenty feet away now, dodg-
ing and kicking at the crazed animal, which strove to
drive its teeth into her legs. Hell, she was a spunky
one—not a single scream, or cry for help.

The constantly leaping dog made a target hard to
hit, and he threw the rock twice and missed each time.
The animal turned on John now, and after he had
kicked it back he retrieved the rock and took a more
careful aim this time. He threw again and managed
to strike the dog on its side, knocking it down and
partially stunning it. The rest was easy—two more
blows and the dog sprawled out dead, with a fine-spun
crocheting of foam and blood showing on its black

muzzle and between its long, white front-teeth. Two
of its legs rose in stiff angles, like crude, insensate
question-marks, and a brown sneer at life had dropped
beneath the short tail. Death had made a small pil-
fering on this flower-strewn field, and if the two re-
maining beings had been dogs, they would have felt
a hushed, superstitious, chilled awe and oppression
and their heads would have been lowered in recognition
of life's darting impermanence—a recognition half-
gravely genuine and half with that great, fearful, senti-
mental show of depression which can and does die in
laughter the moment that danger has been passed and
forgotten. But I am also forgetting—dogs lack the
reasoning powers and the many-shaded emotions held
by human beings: dogs would have scampered off, un-
affected, or crouched beside the stricken one, growling
at smells and sights unknown to human beings. . . .
Fortunate dogs.

John turned around and saw that the girl was sit-
ting in a clump of daisies and crushing some of them
underneath her. One hand was pressed against her
eyes while the other stroked the dress over her left
leg—a dress badly torn by the dog but kept from too
much immodest revealment by the white petticoat un-
derneath. The rear coils of her brownish-black hair
were loosened and studded with upraised hairpins and
wisps of it straggled over her forehead. He walked
up to her and touched her shoulder. Didn't know
quite what to say but had to say something that might
calm her down, or make her talk it off and forget what

a close squeak she'd had. No sex now—just a near-impersonal, bluntly boyish concern—that slightly self-conscious, hat-tilting dimness of egotism which is gallantry, chivalry, and which men often assume but feel less frequently.

"Aw, brace up, kid—the whole thing's over now," he said, as he sat beside her. "He didn't bite you any, did he?"

She removed her hand from her eyes and looked at him. The look on her face rested midway between a smile and a desire to weep with relief, and sometimes twitched into one or the other of these contenders.

"No," she answered. "Least I think he didn't."

She touched her legs to reassure herself. He grinned.

"Don't worry, you'd fe-eel it if he had!"

The smile won in the fight on her face.

"Gee, I can't begin to tha-ank you"—her voice was a drawn-out soprano. "I know he'd have ripped me to pi-ieces if you hadn't come along."

He felt a gruff impulse to disparage his rescue of her —what the heck, he didn't deserve any medals for killing a fool dog. Anybody could have done it. When egotism is delighted with some dramatic victory, in which it appears to repudiate itself, it often strives to disown this victory and thus keep the repudiation intact!

"Aw, don't feel that way—it wasn't much of a trick to knock him stiff. Sure not. You being a girl, you just didn't have muscle enough to do it, that's all."

Her face became more and more shining—not smiling now but humbly beaming over with respect for his modest words and with the bright pain of her desire to repay him somehow in some instant fashion.

"Course, you're a brave man and you don't want to own up to it. Why, I'd have gone to a hospital and maybe di-i-ied if it hadn't been for you."

"Aw, forget about it—please."

"No, how can I? Don't be silly. Why . . . why, I'd do anything on earth just to pay you back a little, honest I would. I'd even let you kiss me now, if you wanted to." . . .

She paused, a little abashed by her last spontaneous words—she could have bitten her tongue off for having said them—and then forcing herself to admit that she had meant them . . . under different circumstances they would have made her feel so common and low, but now it was really unusual and beautiful . . . really. He wasn't a bad-looking boy, either—she hated herself for the observation. No, even if he'd been homely as mud she'd have spoken just as she did. Taken aback by her invitation he stared at her, a sexual measurement stealing for the first time into his eyes. She wasn't so *terribly* pretty, but she had one of the cutest, smallish, tomboy faces he'd ever seen and her slender body, near to medium height, was just a little oddly plump around the waist. Still he hesitated. Kissing her now would be like taking charity in a way, since she was offering her mouth out of kindness and gratitude and not because she had really tumbled for him. Then again, a kiss would have played shuttledore

with his rôle of virtuous, big-father hero which he was
beginning to like very much, although he denied its
existence to himself.

"You don't really want me to kiss you. You just
want to make a present and feel good about it, but
sa-ay, I don't have to get kisses that way. I'm not
bra-agging, but I've got plenty of girls who like me
. . . some."

She felt by turns a little humiliated, and a little
perversely and ashamedly clinging to the hope that
he *would* kiss her in the end, since his unwillingness
would make this kiss nicer, less like he had done it
right off because she'd thrown herself at him. Then
again, this was the first time that she'd ever *asked*
a boy to kiss her, and if this one didn't *now*, she'd feel
painfully snubbed, and it would also be an imputation
on her good-looks. Besides, he *did* appeal to her—she
didn't know just why but . . . who cared? The fact
was enough.

"See here, Mister What's-Your-Name, I don't go
'round making *presents* of kisses to strange boys"—her
voice was spirited but had no sting to it. "I'm sorry
I asked you now so let's forget about it."

Sa-ay, this was a horse of a different color—she was
hurt 'cause he'd treated her like she was a back-num-
ber, and a loose one at that. Aw say, this had to
be rectified, and . . . she *was* a pip. He leaned over,
pressed his hand against the back of her head to pull it
forward, and kissed her mouth several times, neither
lightly nor fervidly but with a boyishly held back well-

you-dared-me-to way. She slid a little away from him and her face was divided—a sulky how-could-you? and a grateful: "But I did bring it on myself, and your mouth tasted peachy." . . .

(Civilization spits on sexual impulses and emotional promiscuity, and calls them unclean, perniciously abnormal, ruinous to the sturdy, healthily compromising, serenely healing structure of homes and knit-together families, but if these structures are indeed so strong and inevitable, how could they be destroyed, or even subverted, by that pagan individualism which civilization denounces as a sickly weakness, a wild futility? The ancient Chinese—lovable creatures—had a proverb which went: "When Hang-Tso called his enemy a loathsome, pus-ridden caterpillar, a stranger in the palace asked: 'Then why do you require an army to step on him?'" The truth is that civilization fears two extremes—paganism on one hand, and all the skepticisms of intellect on the other—but civilization is an involved, shakily hypocritical braggart, who trembles at the slightest sound and jumps at the smallest opposition. Millions of homes and families remain uninvaded, snugly growing, immune to curiosity, but one man need only rise to write a frank union of realism and intellect, or to display those nude, imposing, neurasthenic indifferences called unconventional, and a veritable little bedlam breaks loose in the scene surrounding him. Mawkishly "virtuous," leg-flaunting, crudely scheming tabloids sling their mud and hyperbolic denunciations; cultured critics profane the sacred impersonality of literary analysis and jeer at his mother and sisters, or call him a refuse-vender, or picture him as a monstrous, ludicrous pervert; other critics "discover" that literary themes are inferior when they do not deal with sexually veiled people; men attack him with fists, or boast that they could murder him and receive a vote of gratitude; other men and women on the street recognize his face, from newspaper photographs, and point him out, with frowns and whispers; fellow-authors and literary-patrons remain silent and leave both the man and his creations entirely undefended. O civilization, you are a blustering, teeth-chattering giant afraid of self-made mice, and imaginary poisons in your tea-cup, and fancied banana-peelings on your doorstep. For almost nineteen years you have been rubbing against this boy and girl sitting in a clump of daisies now. They have looked at each other, touched each other a bit, and conversed just enough to feel a tincture of the mental and emotional harmonies possible to their future contacts, and they long to take each other's bodies but scarcely dare to confess this longing even to the most remote vibration within their natures. The loam on which they sit —lumpy and springily redolent with the formless, singing, rudimentary lust of earth; the breezes slapping their faces with a call to happy-go-lucky questing; the swarms of insects feverishly mating in crevices and clod-shelters around their feet; the sky whose largeness cannot perceive the need for cautions and bodices —these are invitations infinitely clearer and more beau-

tiful than the artifices of rooms, with perfumed sheets
and mattresses turning sex into an over-soft, desper-
ately furbished, afraid-to-be-seen luxury, and their
aromas of shame crystallized in darkness, in dim lights
and spuriously delicate privacies and locked doors af-
ter midnight. Sex, bare-breasted, laughing and weep-
ing without concealment, open and undismayed out in
the sunlight and on the weed-matted slopes and hollows
of hills, dells, glades and fields—howl it down, call it
insanely ruinous, laugh at it, remain exquisitely indif-
ferent, you anointed apostles of bound-in, feignedly
complex normality. It will come to pass some day,
or else you and all the human beings on earth will
eventually destroy yourselves, die out under the weight
of the jealous, stifled, grayly defended ugliness that
you have contrived. . . .)

John wanted to kiss her again, wanted to do much
more, but felt that she'd be justified in slapping his
face if he did—girls couldn't be expected to act like
they was bargains and you was picking them up for
next to nothing. As a matter of fact, he'd been forward
enough as it was, mussing her after he'd known her
only a few minutes, and she might not even have been
flirty, in the instant way that "fast" girls had, but just
sort of swung clean out of her usual self by the thing
he had done for her. Well, he'd find out by how she
took it now. She was hanging her head and tugging
at some daisy-centers prisoned near her feet, which
held their stems down. Gee, maybe he'd mortified her
to death.

"You mustn't do that again," she said, raising her head. "I don't want you to think I'm a bad girl, 'cause I'm not. If you hadn't saved me from that terrible brute I wouldn't even have spoken to you."

He smiled inwardly—making out she was even madder than she was, he knew, but still it showed that she wasn't a catch-me-quick one and he had to respect her for it, or rather, part of himself asserted this respect but the other part said: "Aw, the old game's starting again—'I want it but I don't, and I opened my lips and showed that I liked it but I'm going to hand you Cain anyway, and we mustn't be quick about it, mustn't admit it even, but do a lot of teasing and pushing and kidding before we decide, or give in, one way or the other.'" We-ell, he couldn't buck the whole game single-handed, could he? Most every one obeyed it so perhaps it wasn't so wrong after all, perhaps it *should* be respected. Maybe it *was* wrong for boys and girls to be straight, and swift, and honest-talking to each other—both in their refusings and acceptings—though . . . to save his life he couldn't see why.

"See here now, you asked me to kiss you and I did. What's all the fuss about? I liked it fine, and if you didn't, you've got arms and you could have tried to push me off."

She felt angry at his i-impe-erti-ine-ence, and a little farther below, not so angry, and below that, not angry at all. Gee, this boy believed in coming out with things —it was dreadful, and not right, but . . . diverting, and something that somehow she couldn't force herself to dislike. After all, he wasn't talking like he thought she was a flip girl but like they both cared for each other a li-ittle and ought to own up to it, 'spite of the fact that they'd known each other for so short a while and *that* made it reproachful. She didn't know what to say to him now—whether she should make a huge effort to be frank in return, in spite of the self-lowering possibilities, or cling to her tart, ladylike, inviolate coverings.

"Why, I've never *heard* any one talk like you do"—her voice quivered between offended and curious notes. "Never. Don't you think I'm a decent girl?"

"Sure I do—you're not bad just 'cause you let me kiss you."

"Then how could you talk to me like that?"

"Just wanted you to own up you'd taken a liking to me."

"But I haven't—not really."

"You're a liar."

"Wha-at? I'm going to get up and leave you this minute."

"Go ahead then, but just the same I could tell you liked me when I kissed you."

"You're too conceited to li-ive. I haven't the slightest use for you, but I *am* grateful to you 'cause you—'cause you saved my life."

"I'm *not* conceited. I've kissed other girls, 'r tried to kiss them, and I could see darn quick that they didn't care for it. You pressed your lips hard and you was

sort of slow taking them 'way from me, and that's
how I know."

A long pause came, during which a welter of reac-
tions scrambled and whizzed within her—some stamped
out at the very moment of their birth, some allowed
a few seconds of disputed existence, some lingering in
the turmoil and assisting in the death of the others—
a great show of anger at his temerity, with the anger
little more than an obscuring froth; sexual exclusive-
ness piqued at the curtness of his words; bewonder-
ment as to whether she would be degraded if she
admitted that he was telling the truth; the most sneak-
ing of likings for his uncompromising stand; be-
grudged, hungry, self-worried urges to accept him as a
strange and heart-tickling boy; equal urges to put
him in his place by walking away from him, no mat-
ter how much she was beginning to like him; fears
that if she responded to him now he might be encour-
aged to go further and seek to "do her wrong"; equal
fears as to whether she might not be unable to resist
him in such a case; and, in spite of herself, a happy
desire to prolong the "turmoil" which it was in effect
and thus retain the interest which had suddenly been
injected into her flat, sleepy, flower-picking day. Like
many virgins of nineteen, she liked the hoping, easily-
affronted but not-really-injured, secure but insecure,
vampishly pampered, vision-juggling, fire-playing ten-
sions within her condition, and her virginity primped
and kindled itself in preparation for the eventual death,
which had to be denied and courted at the same time,

since any staying allegiance to one or the other would have robbed her of delicious uncertainties, concocted terrors, and titillating enlargements. Still, unlike many virgins of her age, the entire thing to her was not merely a furor that would subside to an underlying acquiescence, or a sheer, animal feeding, the moment marriage, or "illicit" experience, brought an end to the furore's curiosities. She had within her germs of turbulence that would never be completely stilled until her last breath of life came, and her present commotion was their ignorant fertilizer. Her life was to be slashed, momentarily happy, and restlessly darkened again and again. Like John, she belonged to the few Wounded Misfits of this earth—the creatures whose desires are too difficult and yet too straightforward to thrive in the midst of well-armored and more weakly dreaming people, and who lack the articulate talent that could bring them relief from disappointment and libelous misunderstanding.

As John sat and watched the workings on her face, now clouded and now "far off," he began to regret the "fierce" tone in his previous words. He had had a boylike and yet unboylike whim to come clean with a girl for the first time in his life and see what would happen—boylike in its desire to be daring and roughly outspoken, and unboylike in its aroused persistence even after the girl had rejected it with equal obstinacy and he had seen that it wouldn't work. Then it had passed beyond a sexual investigation and had become an explosion of sincerity—of expressing what he thought and letting her walk off in *ten huffs* for all he cared! But now that she hadn't walked off, but was sitting in a mood that seemed to be tormentedly chewing over his words, he felt vindicated and yet uneasy and near-guilty. To call a girl a liar just after you'd met her *was* a pretty nervy stunt at that—he might have shown a little more consideration for her in the wording of his sentiments—"it's not true" or "you're fibbing," or something like that. Girls were softer than boys and they could be hurt by a word, or a slam-bang action, that a boy would only laugh at.

"I don't know what to make of you," she said at last. "I don't even know whether I like you 'r whether I don't. Gee, this is the funniest day *I've* ever had. If anybody'd told me all of this was going to happen, why, I'd have thought they was cra-azy."

"Aw, we're all crazy but we don't know it."

"*You* are, I think."

"You're my sister then."

"D'you *always* talk like this?"

"Sure not—I just got a notion to try it out."

"Well, I *wish* you wouldn't keep it up."

"Like blazes you do. You'd have gotten up and left me long ago if you hadn't *wanted* to talk to me."

"We-el, all right then, I *do* want to talk to you, but I don't see why you have to be so rough to me."

"I'm apologizing, honest. I wouldn't want to hurt you for the world—all I want is to tell the truth."

"Aren't you co-ondesce-endi-ing though."

This time he was the pricked one—she thought he

was swelled-up and just trying to show off in front of her!

"Oh, go to grass," he said. "You pile into me when I'm rough and you wade in when I'm sorry for it. Guess you don't want to be fair to me, that's all."

Her upset condition succumbed to the appeal in his last words—she couldn't help liking him, he was so straight-to-the-point, and gentle-gruff, and disarming. All of her previous rules of procedure became as naught before the new catapultings of his talk. Her parents had drummed warnings into her—she must be on guard against boys, and act like a modest lady, and be sure of their characters, and never give them her photograph, or let them dance too close to her, or speak to them without an introduction—all of the stilted, apprehensive, childish bindings prescribed by billions of parents from biblical days upwards and disobeyed by at least half of their children, while her girl-friends had advised her to be not too careful or too careless but willing to play around with boys until they tried to make a fool out of her (induced her "to go too far"). She had striven to persuade herself that her parents were right and had nodded to the babbling girls while invisibly sticking her tongue out at them—the Lord only knew what some of them did when they went out with boys!—but at the very bottom of her nature these tempests of advice had left her beauteously unmoved. People simply had a *passion* for telling a girl what she should do, and if she said yes, she could keep them quiet with the least effort. Now, all of her second-cousins-to-pouts, and girlish forebodings about nothing and everything, and correct disownings of physical response began to disappear before a boy, who made the spring-time of her heart twitter-twinkle into scherzos of promised summer.

It wasn't his words alone—coming from a blotched hunchback they would have left her attentive against her will, but touched only on the outside skin. An insidious, ruthless, esoteric blend—like the elements in protoplasm, whose identities are known but whose exact proportions hinder the attempts of scientists to create artificial life—must be present, in those cases of immediate appeal which are deeper than the surface of carnality, or the strummings of complimentary social intercourse; a dovetailing of facial lines, vocal inflections, physique, colorings, bearings, and . . . and that rising-in-emergencies, securely oblivious, flesh-whipping, untouched equation, scorned by scientists, psycho-analysts, realists of all kinds—*the soul*.

"Say, I like you," she said, reaching over and grasping his hand.

"Same here. You're a dandy—so darn honest I could eat you."

"Well, if we eat each other up we'll be like the famous cats. That wouldn't do."

They laughed a second—the somehow cruel-kind, instantly unremembering, cleansing laughter of exceptional youth, since the laughter of more ordinary youth is more incessant, weakly spread in chase of atoms not even important to the laughers, and uncleansing. . . .

Their tantrums and peevishness of a few minutes past were now completely forgotten. He bent over and kissed her again and she responded this time as though it were an inevitability. She suddenly rose to her feet.

"Well of all thi-ings—my hat and my pocketbook! I dropped them over there by the fence when that dog came after me. Gee, I hope I haven't lost them."

"Come on, I'll help you find them—don't be afraid."

They walked over to the fence and, after much poking about through the dust-skeined mats of weeds and flowers, located the missing articles.

"My cap's over there by that tree, and it's a nice, shady place. Let's flop down there and talk a while, huh?"

"But I came out here to pick some flowers for my mother—she's sick in bed."

"Gee, that's too bad—what's ailing her?"

"The doctor says its di'betes. You know, sugar in the blood, and she suffers something awful sometimes, but she's getting better now, I think."

"My ma gets rheumatism every so often, and boy, she just can't move a leg when her spells come on. Gee, I wonder whether *we'll* get bunged up like that when we're old people? Seems like life don't want us to be spry and snippy for long, don't it? Almost like God had a grudge against us."

"Oh, you mustn't talk that way about God— He just tests us with afflictions so's we can be stronger and braver," she said, punctiliously, and without a biting belief, repeating the dolorously banal lessons which

she had once heard in occasional visits to a Baptist
Sunday-school during her short-skirt years.

Her family was of the half-heartedly religious kind,
visiting their church only when calamity seemed to
be impending, or when some special catastrophe re-
ported in the newspapers brought home to them the
humanly arbitrary God supposed to stand behind death,
or when their consciences tweaked them with unusual
fervor.

She and John strolled to the tree, still vending the
small-talk with which young people divert, delay, and
yet slowly bring forward the seriousness of their re-
sponses, desiring time in which to adulterate and nurse
the fine quiverings in their hearts—essential children,
made afraid of themselves by the bellowings and tight-
lacings and must-nots of civilization. She sat under
the tree, properly tucking her dress in around her
sweetly slender, prominent-kneed legs, and he dropped
beside her and regarded her for a while. Her forehead
was low but straight; her eyes large, bulging out a
little but not offensively, and with the blackness of
stalactites; her lips were full and closed; her skin was
a dab of brown in cream; and her small nose broadened
at the nostrils, somewhere between pug and aquiline.
Funny, she wasn't pretty at all when he looked closely
at her and yet she made him tingle like he'd been
scrubbed and he could have kissed her till Doomsday.
Prettier girls had made him warm and finger-itching,
of course, but only two of them—one, the prostitute,
Annie—had given him the tiptoey, swirling-'round,

swept-on and yet hating-to-hurt feeling that he had
when his lips touched hers and his arm fitted around
the imperceptibly bribing, delicate-boned, smoothly-
nuanced suppleness of her back. Just a skinny thing
too, mostly, except for her waist. Hell, he couldn't be
falling in love in less than an hour—that wasn't in the
cards: he was too wise-for-his-years to slide for that
gooey stuff. Still, he certainly did get jumpy and lem-
onadish when he touched her and maybe they'd get all
tangled up with each other and hang on for a long
while and light all the fireworks before they split up.
The prospect of a romantic, breathless, cross-my-heart-
and-hope-to-die, story-book affair, with himself cast as
master and able to leave her the moment he became
tired, or another girl attracted him more, appealed to
the cut-throat side of his egotism—the kinship to
cruelty that was too brightly adventurous and innocent
of pain-enjoyment to be quite cruelty itself. Besides,
he said to himself, why think of the future and try
to pin it down and shear it of its supremely teasing
aspects (not his own words but his indefinite wooing
of them)—the present was more overweeningly hot,
befuddling, thickly-flexed.

He was going out with two girls steadily now—two
nights a week with each one. Evelyn Brenner and
Myrtle O'Hara. Sort of half soft on Evelyn but re-
garded Myrtle as a wishy-washy, flirty, jabbering girl,
who smeared on the war-paint till she was a sight,
'spite of her enormously pretty face, and had about as
much brains as a flea—not that girls were supposed to

have bra-ains, but some few of them went even below the accepted level!—and tried to be squeamish and squirmish without really fighting off a boy's advances —just a tart, sought because she *was* exceptionally pretty. Evelyn was *some* different anyway—more like Mary had been. Evelyn didn't wriggle, or plead, but acted like it didn't matter very much to her, though she didn't have Mary's entire lack of feeling and oh-let's-get-busy attitude—he'd probably never in his life meet a girl quite as unmushy and unafraid and down-to-earth as Mary! Even the girls in the Red Light District couldn't quite come up to her, and they did it just for the money mostly. Evelyn could pal around and kid him in the right spots, but she wasn't a girl who set his heart to thumping—just a good sport with no trimmings to her. Then there were others with whom he went out once in a great while—Josephine Mullins, Florence Miller, Irene Hoover—but they were just passable-looking, all-flighty, made-to-order chits, to be called up only when an unexpectedly dateless dance-night loomed ahead. . . . Yes, sir, the track was certainly clear for a rip-snorting, tender-hearted mash and this girl here might be the one to start it.

He had been averting his eyes and now he looked at her again. She was staring at the ground and fiddling with her dress, and a softly troubled and yet beginning-to-be-exalted look was on her face. Wonder what was going on in her mind? She wasn't a dumb-slob by any means—she'd risen to his straight talking with a beautiful straightness of her own in the end and even though she *had* been angry, sillily covered up at first, this was only because she'd never run up against the truth before and it had seemed too much like, we-ell, like taking her clothes off right away and not even blushing about it. He'd had some brass to try it on a good girl, and nearly all of them would have stamped their feet and gone off, or stayed and tried like fury to coax him into playing the fool game again, the ple-ease-don't and ple-ease-let-me idea. Yes, she must be really different from the other girls he knew—something was *bound* to come out of this.

She had been sitting in a fog with rays of light shooting through—conscious moments in which she glanced at his face in that covert, scarcely-second-long way known to some women. He'd have been terrifyingly handsome but for the hump in the middle of his nose, but even that wasn't pronounced and he had large eyes, black like her own—her father said that blue eyes were true eyes, gray eyes were gay eyes, green eyes were mean eyes, brown eyes were clown eyes, and black eyes were smokestack eyes. Her father was a chef now but he'd tried to scribble verses in his youth and even now he often dashed off "poems" in honor of friends who had died or married, or for the menus of the restaurant in which he worked—(sample):

> *Our soup is good, our steak is fine,*
> *Our chicken's simply grand.*

You'll find that Russel's Restaurant's
The best place in the land!

Our pastry smells of heaven—
Yam-pie, blueberry tart.
We pass beyond digestion
And stuff your weary heart.

My, was she going to fall *in love* with this boy, and if she did, what would happen? Rose-buds, ruffled skirts, pot of bluing in the wash . . . cinnamon-cakes, orange garters . . . no more clothes . . . oh, I'm happy . . . spice and ribbons . . . will it hurt me? . . . cloves and ribbons—let it hurt me! He broke the ice.

"Three silver pennies for your thoughts."

"Silver? There aren't any *silver* pennies."

"There are if somebody makes them."

"Silly, then they'd be worth more than pennies."

"So are you."

The wisp of a laugh from her.

"D'you mean it or is it ta-affy?"

"You bet I mean it. You're a sight different from all the girls I know."

"How am I?"

"You're sweet, but you're not a dose of sugar—I mean you don't put it on, see?"

"And what else?"

"Oh, when I told the truth 'bout our wanting to

kiss 'n hug each other you didn't keep on teasing and lying about it, even if you *was* mad at first."

"And what else?"

"You're not as pretty's some girls I know, but gee, when I'm close to *you* I feel like the Fourth of July and *then some*."

"And what else?"

"Sa-ay, this is like a school-exam'—you'll keep me going all afternoon."

They laughed—heart-swollen, dipped-in-visions, pell-mell puffs of laughter.

"Besides, you haven't told me what *you* think of me. I'm not a step-sister, am I?"

"Must I tell you right away?"

"I did."

"We-ell, you're very sincere and you say everything that's on your mind, and I like that."

"And what else?"

"Oh, I think fate must have intended us to meet each other."

"Yes, and what else?"

"Isn't that enough?"

"No, you've left something out."

"What?"

" 'Bout how you feel when we're kissing."

"It's not nice for a girl to talk about *that*."

"Why isn't it? There's no reason to be ashamed of it and I want to find out whether you feel just crazy-happy when you kiss me, because that's the way I feel."

"I'll give you three big guesses."

"Please tell me."

She hung her head. He was so merciless and impatient—he wanted to know *everything,* but if a girl immediately owned up to a boy she might lose him or make him just too careless for words, and besides, she wanted to be courted and bribed and begged and pulled, even when there was no need for it—she had a right to want it.

"I'll tell you the next time."

"No, you'll tell me now or never."

A twinge of anger within her—he was too high-handed.

"All right, it'll be ne-ever then."

He also frowned inwardly—he'd rather move a house than try to get *one* of them to be outspoken. Maybe he'd put her too high in his estimation. Minutes of silence slid on—that quarreling, choked, despairing, grimly make-believe silence, in which youth impersonates the will-power of age and swears that it will never unbend and bids farewell to the object of its desire tens of times but is finally overcome by this desire.

Questions filled her—was he really going to leave her for good; would he give in; should she tell him and throw over all the sweet, dear chasings and words of devotion on pins and needles lest they should be turned down; was he unreasonable, or was she horrid for keeping still; would they never say another word to each other—freezing, marrow-sucking prospect!—

and if they quarreled so often now, did it mean that
they always would? . . . With a wrench, he made
himself speak.

"Did you mean that, about never? Did you?"

He had spoken *first* and that was a heavenly acces-
sion hard to resist.

"I'm . . . not . . . sure."

"Then tell me, d'you get daffy 'n' dizzy when I kiss
you?"

Silence.

"Tell me."

"Y-ye-es"—the word had been wrung out of her
measureless pride, like a whisper born from years
of silence and slaying their influence forever. She
would never be able quite to return to the closed-in,
near-to-bursting, intact ultra-girlishness which had
previously ruled her.

He kissed her again and for the first time she ac-
tively returned the damp clingings of his lips and
the erratic darting of his hands. . . . Then she with-
drew herself and looked at him gladly and reproach-
fully, with the paradox joined by the rapt looseness
of her mouth.

"I've never acted like this to any other boy. I hope
you appreciate that."

"You *bet* I do—I'll stick with you and be true
blue as long's you care for me and . . . and even
longer I guess."

Oh, the vows and pledges of youth, not quite sin-
cere, not quite insincere—to the small extent to which

both adjectives have any meaning—but longing to be the first quality until they almost are, and making themselves so superbly unconscious of the second that it barely survives. She smiled suddenly.

"We're acting like we'd known each other for ye-e-ears and we don't even know each other's na-ames!"

He grinned—the whole afternoon was so unheard-of and upside-down that it might be wise for him to pinch himself. He'd flirted with girls before, in street-cars or public-parks, but he'd never gone this far with them in two hours and he'd never felt more than a cocky, kidding-along, a-little-sneering pleasure at having been able to win their prattlings and quick, fought-for, meaningless kisses, or a who-cares? but smarting-for-a-minute reaction when they repulsed him. It was larger than a cheap flirting-match now—he'd picked up a girl and gone wild about her, and she'd gone the same for him, and they'd fallen into each other's arms like nothing else existed, and the whole thing had had a whirly, fragile-but-unbreakable, too-good-to-be-true appearance. Gee, life sure could jab a man between the eyes and make him stagger 'round like a happy souse—life was a balled-up matter, with plenty of disagreeable work and tussles and rotten knots, but it was also able to make a person feel like honey and cream-cheese. A balled-up thing and no mistake.

She had listened to his pledge with her face and its changings symbolizing the words: "I'd like to believe you but I don't. . . . I do? . . . I don't. . . . I *do*."

Belief is the religion of the blind; the weariness
of open eyes which have stopped against a seemingly
unbudgeable, unbridgeable beauty, ugliness, or slain
question in between; the sold-and-bought-in-a-trice
gewgaw of children; the last candle-sputter of old
people. Belief is the manufactured firmness on which
Life barely manages to stand, midway between sky-
rockets of nerves and hells of pain or enervation.

She believed him—drugs slipping into hearts free-
of-charge; he believed her—when you had a thing *now*
and couldn't dream of becoming tired of it, the now
rose to *always* and your appetite then became more
precious to itself—the nibblings were sweeter when
they fancied that they were dining on inexhaustible
ambrosia. He exchanged names with her—her name
was Elizabeth Harrison. A babble of facts came from
her lips—love turns and points endlessly to details in
its background, as if to say: "Look how much better
I am" or "if I'm dear to you, you'll want to know *all*
about me." She lived in Roseland, a suburb one mile
south of Burnside—roses had grown there thirty years
before factories smoked them out and Greek lunch-
rooms stamped their horrible effigies on menus, walls,
and toilet-entrances. She had quit high-school in her
third year because her father had broken his leg and
money was needed: she was working now in a mil-
liner's shop, as an apprentice; she had a fifteen-year-
old sister but no brothers; her sister was bright and
wanted to be a school-teacher—hated boys and always
scrubbed her face with sapolio when one of them

took her unawares and kissed her; everybody had
praised her soprano voice and she hoped some day to
go on the stage and be a singer, and she was sav-
ing up money to take lessons from an Italian maestro
down-town; she had been going with two other boys,
one of whom lived way out on the West Side, but
they weren't *much*, least not awfully much, and she'd
give them up if John wanted her to.

John's first impulse was to say yes, and then he
wavered—he didn't know whether he was truly in love
with her, but he cared enough for her to want to be
fair. If she threw over her boys and he held on to
one or two other girls she'd be mis'rable then if he
ever left her in the soup—the self-unaware conceited-
ness of youth, imagining itself to be invincible, ir-
resistible, under the guise of consideration and sym-
pathy given to another person.

"Let's not make any promises," he said. "Let's go
out with each other for a week 'r so and see what hap-
pens, huh?"

"All right"—she was piqued and pleased—she'd
never kneel down to him like *this* again, and yet it
was nice to meet a boy who wanted to be sure of
what he felt instead of swearing to be true right off,
to get a girl going.

"You can laugh all you want, but I *am* going on
the stage some time," she said, later on. "Minnie
West, she's a friend of mine, she got me a try-out
at the Roseland Conservatory of Music, and the Big

Man there, he said I had a real sweet, strong voice but I needed a lot of training."

"We-ell, I think *I'm* going to be a dancer. I can do a double-tap slick's a drum! All I need's a good teacher and a chance to break in . . . and sa-ay, wouldn't it be swell if we could get up a team sometime and break into vaudeville. We could put on a clever song-and-dance act, and I'll bet you we'd knock them cold too."

"Wouldn't we, though?"—the old absurd and yet impressive magic of hope and unverified self-esteem shone on her little face.

"I've got fifty dollars saved to take lessons with," she said.

"I'll start saving too, and maybe in a few months we can get into action—maybe less'n that. Sometimes those schools let you in for next to nothing if they think you've got real talents, and then you can sign a contract, 'r something, and agree to pay them back after you're working on the stage."

"Maybe—I never thought of that."

"Well, I'll look up some schools that advertise in the papers, see, and then we'll go down to one 'r two of them and see what they have to say. When'll we go?"

"Well, I work ev'ry day, but I get Saturdays off. Let's make it next Saturday, what d'you say?"

"Sure, that'll be fine."

They went on bandying with hope to feel less submerged, less powerless, more divinely equipped and only marking time before they would demonstrate this divinity, and soon they were disporting themselves behind the footlights of a large theater in the Chicago Loop District—oh, a shiny, thrice-elegant, tuneful, supreme bird of a theater—while they went through the difficult stunts of trillings and tappings as though they were the veriest flutterings of habit, and flung side-splitting jests at each other with perfect seriousness—all in the day's work, you know—and accepted the salvos of applause afterwards, as though they liked this appreciation but were so terribly used to it. . . .

Youth, youth, you are the brief space in which life, with erect flesh and unrestricted limbs and the beauty of ignorant courage, towers above the refuse-laden morals, sticky lies, "altruistic" bastinadoes, wormy cautions, tumors of common-sense eating into the uncommon sportiveness of dreams, and stealthy guzzlings conceived by older people, who are gripped by the great *fear-and-envy* virus within their largely defeated days. Exceptional youth perpetuates itself and is contained in exceptional old age, but the main transitions go on undisturbed. . . .

John told her of his plan to become a peanut-hawker at the Big League Ball Park—it was a spine-shrinking descent from his dreams of twinkling fame and his assertions of unusual talent, but he sought to laugh it off and make it a voluntary lark—the potentially great man, idling a little now because he was so sure of the wreaths that would fall on him later

on. Besides, didn't *she* work in a millinery shop?—
when people were starting out with no money they had
to take orders, mop slop, and do everything, but they
could avenge themselves when they got to the top. . . .

People are born with widely varying degrees of poetry
within them—poetry, the invisible, hurt-unto-death-but-
never-dying, eviscerating, pain-large recklessness,
where caprice and logic become friendly with the dis-
covery *that one horizon eludes both of them.* John and
Elizabeth were not innately fitted for the rôles of
vaudeville-dancer and singer, and not even deeply in
love with these rôles. They had grasped them as the
only perceptible outlets of expression in their crimped,
penny-ruled, small-vocabularied, flatly tinted environ-
ments—an untutored, self-shaky ache that longed to
escape into the rewards of an outside world, regardless
of what shape this fleeing might take—anything,
anything to rise above the sameness of a few streets ob-
scurely walked upon, and the expectations and warn-
ings of families, whose only dreaming was a sentimen-
tal stretching-out sometimes between hours of toil, and
the thrill-less, pseudo-proper observances in parlor and
yard, where flesh was the bogy-man waiting for mar-
riage to turn it to a decent, permissible pleasure! They
were at the bottom-scale of poetry—inarticulate and
self-beclouded members. *The bottom and the top may
sometimes change places, but the degrees in between
never move, never alter. . . .*

"Say, why don't you take in the game to-morrow?
I'll have to breeze down 'bout noon and hook the job.

but I could meet you at one of the gates afterwards
. . . and say, free peanuts for you, hon', if I can spot
you in the stand."

Her heart jumped at the idea of going, not because
she liked baseball, or understood it thoroughly, but
because it would be an aimless, gingery, warm-aired
celebration of her meeting with him and the bubblings-
over now inside of her, and the shouting tension of
the rooters would harmonize with her feelings—every-
body yelling and so glad to be alive. Then a cloud
took the unripe glistenings off her face—gee, it would
cost at least a dollar, and she had to buy new shoes on
Monday, and oh da-arn, sometimes she thought that
life was just an empty pocketbook daring a girl to be
happy! Her silence puzzled him.

"What's the matter—can't you go?"

She groaned to herself—he mustn't know that she
couldn't afford it.

"O-oh, I don't care much for baseball."

"Please, I *wish* you'd come. I won't mind working
hard to-morrow if I know you're going to meet me right
afterwards."

"It's sweet of you to say that, John, but . . . I
guess I'd better not."

He darkened over—she had already pledged herself
to another lad and was just playing hookey from him
—an afternoon of sneaking, unmeant kisses and kid-
dings. Oh the trigger-swift, bruised-by-shadows, man-
ifold misunderstandings of youth, which mistakes its

own captious impatiences for the cleverest of perspicacities.

"Well, don't forget to tell him all about me"—he frowned up at the sky.

"Hi-i-im?"

"Sure, the boy you're going out with to-morrow—I know."

"Please, John, I haven't any other beau—not a *real* one anyway."

"Then why can't you come to the game to-morrow and meet me afterwards?"

She moaned to herself and rapidly ran over a list of possible excuses—her mother's illness; seeing a girl-friend; having to visit relatives . . . no, they'd all sound lame because she hadn't said them before—sound like an after-thought. She couldn't blame him for not understanding—boys always moved straight ahead and never looked to the left or right—and she would have sunk down to her shoes if he *had* understood—it was so hateful to seem like a pauper. She'd have to spend the money and somehow wheedle two dollars out of her pa—he *was* a big-hearted man in many ways but had to scrimp so when he was young that he couldn't get out of the habit now.

"What, uh, what does it cost to get in? I just want to be sure to take enough with me."

Insight split him in a flash.

"Oh say now, don't let the price worry you none. I was going to treat you to the game all the time and I'll be real mad if you don't let me, I will."

"What makes you think I was worrying?"

"Oh I don't know—I thought you might be."

"No, indeed, I can pay my own way and I'm going to."

He thought it over and decided on a bold shot—his instinct had seen through her pitiful little sham and he felt that it had to be smashed, though not unkindly.

"Listen here, when two people care for each other there shouldn't be no false pride between them. I don't give a darn if you're poor's a mouse, 'cause I am too and we're both in the same pickle. I've got four dollars now and I can spare them, so you're going to let me treat you, that's all. You just stop hiding 'round when there's no need to hide . . . please."

His words had taken the sting out of the situation and made them both two vagabonds with arms linked and pennies compared, scoffed-at—how she admired his straight, undressed, rudely infectious way of getting to the point of everything. It made her own qualms and quirks and quandaries seem like such worthless maneuverings.

"You're just the loveliest boy I've ever met"—they kissed each other again and joined the plundering of hands.

Soon they were walking down the railroad-tracks— she, with her bunch of wild-flowers, and her torn, dark blue dress, and her slender body so ineffably poised between sunrise lust and ethereality, and her brownish-black hair once more pinned into the bunches which seem to epitomize civilization's formal patterns;

and he, in his cheap suit of dark cotton-serge, and his gray cap with the peak slanting up over his dark brown hair, and the muscle-buds on arms and chest, and the scowl of great "wisdom" on his face. . . .

John and Elizabeth parted with a lingering hand-pressure—they were on the corner of Ninety-third Street and Cottage Grove Avenue now, and the pastoral, wind-tossed, madrigaled freedom of flowers, weeds, and the unconcerned shadows of a tree, had given way to a one-story, wooden ice-cream parlor, with its rusty screen-door, tattered gray awning, and fly-specked boxes of bonbons in the window; a cinder sidewalk that crunched beneath their feet; a two-story wooden building with a saloon underneath and that unearthly resemblance to an open-jawed leer, which painters sometimes catch; a three-story apartment-house of red-painted brick, with a sickly frilliness of dirtily pale curtains in the windows, and a heavy, tin, brown-painted cornice on the roof that saved the house from looking entirely like an overlarge bin; and an empty lot with clinker-heaps, cans, newspapers, and assorted débris dumped into its depression, and with a bill-board proclaiming the virtues of Grand Rapids furniture, canned fruit, and shoe-polish. . . . People gave the boy and girl hard, what-have-you-been-up-to looks as they scanned her torn, a little crumpled dress, and a thickly vestured, intrusive, ready-to-pounce, pseudo-decorous atmosphere hung everywhere, except on the corner-saloon, where grimy laborers filed in and out with many a lurch and oath. John and Elizabeth had the suddenly crowded-in daze of a boy and girl yanked from the shaggy privacy of a field and placed once more amidst pointing fingers, implications of sin, virulent modesties, dismaying barriers, and she wondered a little whether she hadn't been wrong and bad out there in that field, while he told himself that he might have gone slower with her since she was such a decent peach of a girl—when they were fast, or leading-on, then they had no one to blame but themselves, but this girl was in a class by herself. The discountenancing artifice was momentary. The singing, heads-up, unthinking spilling-over of their youth could not be cheated so easily, and their chemical magnetism toward each other, spiced by a goodly dash of mental liking, changed their feeling of rashness and made it seem a quieter inevitability. Gosh, when you were gone on each other you stayed that way, whether it was right or wrong. . . .

John walked down Ninety-second Street to his home four blocks away. Sometimes the walk was cement, sometimes beaten earth, and again cinders between horizontal planks, and slimly acquiescent poplar-saplings stood along the walks, and the street was unpaved, with hollows and ruts that changed to a semi-quagmire after a heavy rain. The houses were never higher than two stories and an attic and they came in four, slightly differing varieties—porchless, with conical, shingled roofs; small verandas and flat roofs covered with tarpaper; high front steps leading to the second story, with the first half as low as a basement; two-story bricks with wooden back-porches—little shiftings in a general form, whose vitiated huddle of angles and parsimony of flat fronts conveyed a Judas-hint of that brutally utilitarian camouflage of the spirit which had made them just enough space to live in, just enough variety of line to prevent the structures from looking utterly like kennels, or warrens. Yet the front and back yards were singularly spacious in their contrast to the houses and some of them had flower-beds of nasturtiums, jonquils, peonies, gladioli, dahlias, preachers'-fleece, or truck-gardens in the rear. . . .

Men hewed log-cabins and stockades in the wilderness because they had to tighten up in the face of vast dangers, and an uncertainty as indefinably ever-present as the rustle of billions of leaves overhead, and the clearer menace of wolf and panther, but the hunched-up, smugly-angled houses in city-suburbs of humble laborers and small bosses—with here and there a scroll-work, or trellis, standing like the fraction of a whim to be "fancy"—represent a different concentration—imagination become small and hard; a thriftiness of spirit that hoards boards as well as pennies; and hearts turning-in with the years and rarely expanding. Yet nothing pertaining to human beings is ever quite one-colored, or uni-formed. The yards and the occasional gardens in the front and rear of the houses came from a beaten-down, dirtied, barely breathing impulse toward color, grace, roominess.

John dropped a hand upon the wire fence in front of his house and vaulted into the yard—youth, proud of its body and showing off to itself. The house was a two-story, six-room structure owned by his father but heavily mortgaged. It had a small front-porch and the three-foot symptom of an attic, and a V-shaped roof, and it was thickly painted in dark green and white, since it had to be an ever-shellacked advertisement of the elder Musselman's trade. John walked to the rear and tramped into the kitchen—entering through the front and tracking dirt in hallway and parlor was an offense comparable to murder in this household, for, although the Musselmans were Germans two generations removed from the native land, they had that truly Teutonic, middle-class passion for tidiness, cleanliness incarnate, which is a mark of physical poverty polishing its few possessions (exceptions exist in all races!). The family had gathered in the kitchen—Julius washing at the kitchen-sink, Elsa putting dishes on the table, Augusta, the mother, puttering over the gas-range, and Albrecht, the father, poring over an evening paper. . . .

The condition of normality, when it lacks those educations and borrowed cultures which provide it with *an assumed complexity,* is always an inwardly flabby and outwardly sturdy compromise. With its moderations and cheatings of spirit must go an attitude of voluntary choice and control, since otherwise it would become too much a prisoner unto itself, and so it adopts the simple device of being unrestricted in profession rather than in fact—mean walls become sacred protections; repressions are called girded wis-

doms; boresome proprieties change to the graceful
niceties of life; sexual curiosity becomes "unclean"
and degenerate; unsparing candor is dismissed as a
hate-filled falsehood; and carefree nudity alters to a
barbaric deterioration. As the late Stuart Pratt Sher-
man pointed out—the last of the self-aware, self-sub-
duing conservatives in this country!—we are born
abnormal and normality must be slowly and often
painfully *acquired*. In salons, studios, and upper mid-
dle-class apartments, this acquisition, this false-face
assuming all the poses of restrained naturalness, can
take on those mannerisms, modes and amenities, which
lend it a seeming variety and charm, but in places such
as the Musselman kitchen it lacks these rescuing pol-
ishes and obscuring twists of vocabulary, and stands
forth in all of its essential dullness, chained mirth,
weakness of spirit, envious fears, and impulses crushed
for the most part but occasionally extracted by some
irresistible temptation.

(Come, critics and laymen—rail at this attack on
"respectability"; or say that "it wouldn't be interest-
ing even if it were true," in the manner of people-
about-town trifling with the coin-clinking sportiveness
of night-clubs and the latest style in golf-tweeds; or
call it the fanaticism of an inverted Bourgeois, who
assails the objects which he secretly resembles; or lug
in your worn-out, invented decencies and honors; or,
better still, ignore it, since you can change neither
yourselves nor the individual who has written these
words.) . . .

Augusta was a hypochondriac with a sponge-like body. Illnesses, feigned or exaggerated, could place her in bed, relieved of the endured but never palatable tedium of that housework which she had known for twenty years; deliciously waited-upon and humored; and with a sweetly lazy guiltiness firm on her really tired back against the feather-mattress. If Augusta had been a dyed-in-the-wool German-American house-wife—a woman held by that trampled, least-dreaming, fairly contented condition known as average—she would have scoured her pans as an artist polishes off his canvases, and swept her floors with a righteous energy, to which the dirt would have been a commodity left by the Devil, and washed her clothes with the élan of one doing her mite to perpetuate the always threatened purity of the world (subconsciously, of course), but the trouble with her was that she was neither a full-fledged dreamer nor a practical monkey—an indeterminate, hidebound but chafed, blinkered creature . . . confusion on a small scale with few words within her to mold it . . . itchings and cracklings still darting from a bottom-numbness of heart . . . caring now for little but *rest*—heaven-saturated, limb-soothing rest—and the pleasure of issuing small commands to her children and seeing them jump to the sound of her words . . . and sometimes, but not often, worries and angers that could bring back a reviving tingle of life after days of near-inertia in bed, with the beloved medicine-bottles standing on a stool to the left of the bed and fondled when she was tired of reading some cheap magazine.

Did she love her children?—the old yes and no invariably contend within such a question. Flesh-loyalty, that visualizes the child as a seemingly separate but still invisibly joined part of the original body, was ·there of course, with all of its selfish refusals to admit any cleavage of interest, or purpose, between parent and child; and patted feelings when the children did something that sanctified the hindrances and cares which had invaded her after the first, few, stolen rogueries of youth; and a pride in the sturdiness of their bodies, which made the "weakness" of her own all the more remarkable for having given birth to it— all these things, yes, but also dissents and wearinesses! A little hatred because these children had drained her of her youth and her gaddings-about before marriage —hushed, shiveringly stepped-on, disguised by tens of justified irritations when "they did something wrong," but there nevertheless—and a selfishness prone to adore them when they were obedient and affectionate-tongued and loathe them when they dared to oppose their wills or go off on forbidden trips, verbalities. . . .

Augusta had abundant brown hair threaded with gray and bound to a rising, puff-ball effect when she was out calling, or had visitors, and pinned in a loose bag against the nape of her neck and upper back when she was alone with the family. Her face was a souvenir of the kind that Victorian houses used to have on the mantelpiece—the porcelain face of a shepherdess under a glass bowl, with a chip taken from the long nose, another chip from the unfirm chin, another from the warped bud of a mouth . . . mishandled by time: skin of the lack-luster, grained smoothness that suggests a mineral compound . . . and *then* a pair of eyes demolishing the previous metaphor—a pair of eyes like madness teetering between the third and fourth dimensions . . . a pair of brown eyes as remotely unerring as light-years'—a pair of eyes that knew nothing of nine-tenths of her and revealed the other tenth forever gleaming on the verge of a crucifixion . . . a pair of eyes that held the clue to Augusta Musselman. A joker behind the universe—not knowing who he is, we invent crudely comical images of him—had slipped a dash of poetry and soul-knowledge into an otherwise sorry and witless servant-girl . . . and she had transmitted it to one of her children—John . . .

Albrecht was a chunk of hairy muscles; an upstanding ruff of black hair; a stubby nose with a wart on the left nostril; the small black eyes of a respectable scavenger . . . the catalogue is too wearisome. Matters of flesh-molding are Puckish misadventures—the great literary critic's face is identical with that of an old-clothes man met on Delancey Street, and the features of a United States President are reflected in those of a subway-guard. . . . Albrecht was a peasant, with a streak of priest and a stronger one of flesh-rollicker. Albrecht went down on his knees every Sunday at the Lutheran Church but on the eve-

ning of the same day he could be seen peeking at the
three, blind (turned-down) cards in an auction-
pinochle game to win fifty cents—the old jackal-and-
angel division which makes human beings such
preposterous, split-up, self-stabbing, lachrymose crea-
tures. Albrecht was unfaithful to his wife twice a year,
around Christmas and the Fourth of July, when the
holiday spirit and increased *schnapps* would enflame
the remains of his libido and he'd get his friend, Joe
Sloan, the owner of a corner saloon, to telephone a
house in South Chicago and have one of the girls come
over to a room above the saloon, in Sloan's bachelor-
apartment. The matter had to be handled with great
care and secrecy since Albrecht would rather have cut
his right hand off than have the family find out about
these slippings. Such a discovery would have shat-
tered forever his two-thirds sincere pose of a moral,
orally snow-white, flesh-forbidding father, and his chil-
dren would have proceeded to run loose then and throw
his own failings up to him if he raised a hand (in
his fears) . . . u-ugh. . . . "The sins of the fathers
are visited unto the children and their children"—
Albrecht took this line with a groaning seriousness and
tried hard to avoid his semi-annual descents, but it
was physiologically impossible. He had been a catch-
as-can blade before his marriage, and the peasant-faun
within him was a shade more real than his godly side
because it had that much less fear—the difference be-
tween a single, spontaneous forward-step and a de-
liberate retirement. . . . Albrecht prayed to his God

to be forgiven, and the miraculous leniency was ten-
dered the moment he rose to his feet, since prayer is
only the crying-out resort by means of which imagina-
tion achieves its ends through the invention of an
outside, rescuing agency.

Julius was so like his father that he might have been
mistaken for a much younger brother—medium height;
a little broader in the shoulders; much the looked-up-to
bully of his family and often spared even by the
father, since he earned thirty-five a week at the age
of twenty-one and that was regarded as a distinction
and proof of ability that demanded an almost abased
response—if he had made the money as a business-
man, or teacher, they would have been unstirred, but
his mechanic's fusion of strong man and good pay-
check made them worshipers—all except John, who
was neither devoted nor hostile . . . his brother was
a regular skate and generous, too, but "a damn sight
too bossy," and with nothing different in him, noth-
ing to hate or chase after . . . just a good, plain
working-stiff, who was crowing 'cause he made big
money and could take girls to high-class theaters
down-town and buy a diamond ring on the installment-
plan—ten down and five a week . . . if you couldn't
own a thing outright, the hell with it . . . the dreamer
and the son-of-earth often do not come to death-grips
for years, for a lifetime, since the former may be too
embryonic, or abstracted, to proclaim himself to the
near-sighted eyes of the latter. Some kindling of
chance, some disrobing and clashing caused by the

unexpected advent of another person, is needed to
make the potential adversaries aware of their aliena-
tion.

Julius thought that his brother was a pain in the
neck sometimes because he liked red ties and sleeve-
bands, and a whipper-snapper who didn't know his
place, but on the whole a good-enough guy, whose
baseball-playing and fence-hurdling abilities had to
be respected and whose temper was after all only the
spunky lack of yellow so marked in the Musselman
array. Wasn't in his family's blood to take back-
spouting from no one, and he'd have had little use for
his brother if he hadn't fought back with him. They'd
had a real scrap once because he'd poked one of John's
girls in the side and she hadn't liked it, and he'd licked
John but not before John had given him a pair of
shiners and a bloody nose. They'd shaken hands and
made up afterwards but . . . a trace of the grudge
hung on. John was beginning to use a four-syllabled
word now and then, and getting books at the Public
Library branch on Eighty-seventh Street in Dauphin
Park, and cleaning his fingernails all the time—dis-
tasteful symptoms to Julius, who considered them the
first, faint signs of a weakling's emerging. Still,
family loyalty, even though it may be more a creation
of habit than inclination, cannot be broken down by
preliminary smartings and tappings. Julius excused
his brother on the ground of his being a kid just fool-
ing around, and delayed the birth of formidable anger.

Elsa—a dimpled, unawakened, harum-scarum kid,

with her mother's nose but a fuller mouth, and with blue eyes that came from no perceptible source and were ablaze with a carnality as yet innocent of its identity, and a stout, twenty-year-old body despite her sixteen years. Somehow, her father's and mother's diverging natures, meeting within her, had died to form a third entity that was prankish, insensitive, and yet amazingly honest—a cutting-up self that might be shoved into respectable marriage but would always kick the traces in some physical way, since Elsa was entirely nervous flesh, with mind and soul scarcely more than sanguine accommodations. . . .

JOHN [*hanging his cap on a nail beside the pantry*]. 'Lo folks.

[*A grunt from his father, and an inquiring grin from his sister, and "h'lo" from* JULIUS.]

AUGUSTA. Where was you all afternoon? Where?

JOHN. Sitting under a tree by the tracks, ma.

AUGUSTA. Sitting under a tre-ee? Is that all you got to do? Is it?

JULIUS. Ye-ep, that's what I say—he's got it pretty soft, pre-et-ty-y so-oft.

JOHN. Aw, slow down. I'm going to work at the Ball Park to-morrow.

ELSA. What doing?

JOHN. Peddling peanuts—what d'you think?

ELSA [*titteringly*] Pe-eanu-uts . . . peenie-wee-hie pe-eanu-uts.

JOHN. You heard me.

ELSA. Who'd of thunk it. Gees, can't you get a better job than that, Mister Smartie?

JOHN. Aw, I'm only killing time till the summer goes. I'll do something big this fall, you wait 'n see.

AUGUSTA. Something big, is it? So what is this something big? Suppose you tell your ma about it.

JOHN. I'll keep it under my lid.

AUGUSTA [*with tender derision*]. Ach, you got nothing to keep there but your hair, I tell you.

JOHN. Sure, that's what you always say, but that don't bother me none *a*-tall.

ELSA [*singing the words scoffingly*]. Johnny wouldn't te-e-ell, 'cause he didn't kno-o-ow.

JOHN. The hell I won't.

ALBRECHT. John, you know I don't stand for no cussing in the house. I don't want no he-elling around here.

JOHN. Oh, all right, pa.

ALBRECHT. I've told you a hundred times if I've told you once.

JOHN. A-all ri-ight, I'm stopping.

JULIUS. Better listen to what pa says.

JOHN. Listen yourself—I can get along with *my* ears.

[*The family sits down to eat.*]

AUGUSTA. We-ell, I'm still waiting to hear about what you got in mind when the fall comes in, I'm still waiting. Do I got to ask you sixty times?

JOHN. Aw, ma, Julius 'n Elsie are always making me mad. I'll tell you, ma. I've got two things in mind

—either I'll work my way through college, see, 'r else I'll study tap-dancing and go on the stage.

AUGUSTA. Go to college? Go on the stage? We-ell, I don't know. I can't see much money in things like that, but it's not the money exactly. No, it's not the money, it's not. I don't know whether you're cut out for them things. If I thought you was I'd never stand in your way, I never would.

JULIUS [*waving a potato-dumpling on a fork to emphasize his remarks*]. Aw, I know, all you want to do is get out of working hard. You come down to the roundhouse with me Monday morning and I'll get you a man's job, I will.

JOHN. The heck you will.

JULIUS. Ye-es, the heck I will. We need wipers and oilers and we're paying sixteen a week. Sixteen smackers, get me?

JOHN. Ye-es, I get you, I get you, but it's going right into one ear and out of the other. I'm going to amount to something and make a name for myself 'fore I'm through.

ELSA [*keeping up her sing-song badinage*]. Johnny doesn't like his na-ame so Johnny'll make a-an-no-othe-er.

JOHN. Ah you shut up—nobody's talking to you.

JULIUS [*skin-scraped*]. D'you want me to tell you something? You've got a bunch of fancy notions but you'll wind up working hard for a living just like the rest of us, you will, and you'll be damn glad to do it.

JOHN. Sure, I'll work for a living, sure, but gees,

you fellows seem to think there's no way of working 'cept being a mechanic, 'r a painter, 'r a hodcarrier, 'r something like that.

ALBRECHT [*sniffing at the possible aspersion against the colossal though little appreciated dignity of his trade*]. Now, now, them's honest ways of earning a living. Don't turn up your nose at them.

> [ALBRECHT *goes on to assert that a house-painter doesn't mess with other people's refuse, like a plumber; and doesn't spoil his appetite in a dirty kitchen, like a short-order cook; and doesn't have to lift his own weight and more, like a steam-fitter or a furniture-mover; and doesn't come nigh to sawing his arms off, like a carpenter.* ALBRECHT *is launched on his favorite supper-discourse but* AUGUSTA *lets it run only twenty seconds this time.*]

AUGUSTA. Yah, I know, it was fine to be a painter, I know, so maybe then you could pay the furniture-bills what come in the mail this morning? You think maybe you could?

ALBRECHT [*blabbering under his breath*]. Aw . . . ri' . . . s'nough . . . s'nough.

> [*This was no way of helping him keep the respect of his children, no way at all.*]

JOHN. As I was saying now, I'm no bum, no, sir, and I'm not afraid of working either. If a fellow's on the stage now, 'r if a fellow studies like blazes, well, he's got no cinch of it either. All I say is, there's more than one way of working in this here world!

AUGUSTA.   Maybe you got right . . . maybe.

[AUGUSTA *liked him a good inch more than she
did the others, because he had her nose and
eyes and because her soul said hello to him
without her knowing it.* ELSA'S *religion was to
pitch into* JOHN, *without malice and just to
entertain herself by getting a rise out of him,
for she liked the spirited way in which he took
up for himself.*]

ELSA.   Oh, yeah, yeah, maybe the moon's made of
green cheese too. I know what's eating Johnny, I
know. He can't get over that ten he won down at The
Star 'n Garter this winter.

JOHN.   Who can't?

ELSA.   You can't.

JOHN.   Well, suppose I can't? Didn't the stage-
manager down there tell me I had a future as a dancer?
Didn't he?

ELSA.   How do I know—I didn't hear it.

JOHN.   No, but you heard the whole audience clap-
ping like thu-under when I got through.

ELSA.   O-oh go-o o-on, the rest of them was so
sti-inky you couldn't help but win, 'cause you was just
a little better than they was, see, smartie?

JULIUS [*grinning mightily*].   I'll *bet* that was it.

JOHN.   Well, Jule, if you're so anxious to bet now,
I'll bet you I'll be tapping in some show down in the
Loop inside of a year, 'n maybe less.

JULIUS.   I'll take you up on that.

JOHN.   You will, huh?

JULIUS. Sure I will—how much d'you want to put up? How much?

JOHN. Well, I've only got a five-spot on me now so I can't bet with cash, see, but I'll bet you twenty and shake hands on it right 'fore everybody here. That's what' *I'll do.*

JULIUS. Noth-thing stir-ring—I ain't betting on no promises. Cash talks with me. Whenever you got twenty dollars you want to *throw* away, you give them to pa and I'll put up the same.

JOHN. All right—don't trust me then. You're just saying that 'cause you think I won't raise the twe-en', but you'll find out, you will.

JULIUS [*smiling negligently*]. Seeing's believing with me—I'm from Missouri. I'll just wait till you fork it over.

ELSA [*really backing* JOHN, *now that it's come to an issue*]. Well, I think he *will*, so the-ere.

AUGUSTA. I don't like all this betterei now, I don't like it one bit. First thing I know you'll all be betting on the horse-races and betting heavy on the cards and betting on them horse-shoe games over in the lot behind the house. Keep your money . . . *better.*

ALBRECHT. Say, Goosta, was this a joke yet? Better not be no better—heh, heh—that's a good one.

[ALBRECHT, *thinking uneasily of his pinochle-
losses, is trying to laugh the subject off.*]

AUGUSTA. You, with your old a-au-uction games down at Sloan's all the time, you keep quiet now. I'd like to have all you lost down there, I'd like to.

ALBRECHT. Oh, go 'way with that lo-o-osing, lo-o-sing. According to you I never win.

AUGUSTA. If you do, I never see much of it.

ALBRECHT. When it comes to memory, Goosta, you're nix. I didn't come home and give you half two weeks ago. I didn't, huh?

AUGUSTA. Two weeks ago?

ALBRECHT. Yes, two weeks ago. Just after the doctor says you could get up from the bed.

AUGUSTA. A-all ri-ight, so you *did* give me then, but how often does it happen? How often, I ask you?

ALBRECHT [*throwing up his hands*]. Once a year —have it your way—once a year.

[*The parents rise from the table and the other three continue to talk, as they linger over the coffee and cheese-cake.*]

JULIUS [*to* JOHN]. Big doings over at the Masons' Hall to-night. Six-piece band and all the beer a fellow can slide down. You going?

JOHN. Yep, I'm dated up with Myrtle O'Hara. I'm not crazy 'bout going with her though. If you want, I'll let you 'phone her up and tell her I'm sick, see, and you want to know if she'll go to the dance with you. She'll do it all right, she'll be only too glad to, 'cause she can't hook a partner with the blow-out just a couple of hours off.

[*This variety of self-entrenched, "thre' pence" deception is not habitual to John but, wrapped up in Elizabeth, he regards his date with Myrtle as an emotional misdemeanor.*]

JULIUS. Sa-ay, any time you pitch one of your girls at me I'm looking in the woodpile. What's the matter now, did you have a falling-out with her?

JOHN. Nope, I'm just plain tired of taking in her gab.

JULIUS. Tired nothing. Guess she wouldn't come across and you want to play something easier, I know.

JOHN. Hey, mind how you talk with Elsie sitting here, will you?

ELSA. Little ba-aby E-elsi-ie . . . ha ha. I wasn't born yesterday, and don't you think I was. I know what it's all about, apsy dappy, and I'm going to be some cut-up the minute ma lets me go out without you two bums hanging around and spoiling everything.

JULIUS. We-ell, don't you cut up too much—I won't have no sister of mine getting herself talked about!

ELSA. You *won't*, huh?

JULIUS. You heard me.

ELSA. I will if I want to, but I don't want to . . . not yet anyways.

JULIUS. You will like hell.

ELSA. Aw, go chase a lizard. You and John can do what you want, but a gi-i-irl, she's got to be different.

JULIUS. Sure, nobody cares what a boy does long's he settles down afterwards but a girl's got to watch her p's 'n' q's 'r she'll have a bad name in a second, yes, sir.

ELSA. O-oh, I se-ee, then all the girls you and John go out with, they've a-all got go-ood names and that's why you take them out, isn't it? Specially Myrtle O'Hara and Fanny Burke.

[JULIUS *wilts beneath her sarcasm, but feels himself forced to stand his ground—'no man wants his sister to be like the girls he takes and laughs at afterwards and describes their good points and how to approach them to his cronies in the corner saloon.'*]

JULIUS. Hell, no. . . . Well, suppose I do want you to be head 'n' shoulders above the girls I go 'round with—what of it? What of it? When I get ready to *marry*, I'll throw 'em all over and pick out a decent girl, a decent girl, see, like I want you to be.

JOHN. Yeah, Jules is right.

[JOHN *isn't against his sister, but a little puzzled, a little self-accusing, and siding with his brother only because it helps to dismiss the whole, vexingly-angled question.* ELSA *is simply amused— the old fakes, wanting to hog all the fun and then ma-a-arry when they were tired of running around, while a girl had to sit down and do needle-stitching, she supposed, and wait till one of them got ready to propose to her, and even then, if she didn't love him, why, she'd just keep on waiting—what was time to her? A good joke, boys, but* not *for little* ELSA!]

ELSA. Now isn't that nice, isn't it? That's just

exactly what *I'm* going to do. Just it. I'll have a good
time with lots of boys, see?—oh, lots 'n' lots of them—
and *then* I'll put the soft pedal on and I'll marry a
nice, decent boy, and o-oh, I'll be a da-ai-isy of a
wife to him. You see how it is.

JULIUS. You got it all mapped out, huh? All
mapped out? Well, we'll see about it. You're in for
a heck of a squabble if *you* try to run loose, and I'm
going to tell ma what you said, what's more.

ELSA [*knowing that he wouldn't tell*]. Go ahead
and tell her, snitchy-cat. See who cares.

[JOHN *is listening with a four-partied fight going
on within him. He doesn't want his sister to
be a fast one pawed around by this guy and
that, but if the brothers of the girls he went
with had the same idea, what was the answer
then?—thousands of brothers fighting thou-
sands of other brothers and none of them really
carrying out what they claimed to believe in,
for if it was wrong for your sister then it ought
to be wrong for all the other sisters. There
was a jaw-breaker! Seemed like nothing mat-
tered to any one 'less it struck home to them.
If he saw a guy touching his virgin-sister with-
out holding back, he'd get hot under the col-
lar, but when he did the same thing to another
girl of the same kind, he never worried about
her family's feelings, did he? Then again,
seemed like there was nothing but lying con-
nected with sex—"don't tell a soul," "hope ma*

and pa don't find out," "is the door locked?"
married men sometimes untrue to their wives—
he knew a good six in Burnside alone, and they
trotted to church every Sunday too, "always
pull your dress down but roll your eyes if you
like him," "never go near a prostitute"—if pros-
titutes were so bad why weren't they all locked
up, or driven out of business? "Yes, take a
woman now and then but see that you use the
proper precautions"—this from the family-doc'
himself! "Don't read that book, it's too dirty
for you, but I'll read it because I'm grown up
and grown-ups are allowed to read dirt." . . .
Hidings and lies; a blustering, tricky, fair-speak-
ing, ravenous rigmarole (the thought was his
but not the exact adjectives), and if any one
could make head or tail of it, they were wiser
than he was.]

JOHN. Aw, it's all a puzzler to me. People just
don't practice what they preach—just don't do it, that's
all. You go ahead and do what you want to, Elsie.
It's your business and nobody else's. That's what I
think.

ELSA. Good for you, Johnny. You stick on my
side.

JULIUS. That's no advice to be giving a girl like
Elsie here. That's no advice. D'you want her to turn
out like Myrtle, 'r Josie, 'r any of the skirts we know?
D'you want her to turn out like *them*, huh?

ALBRECHT [*who has entered the kitchen and caught JULIUS's last sentence*]. Turn out like what?

[*The three silently look at each other, with a compact of concealment on their faces and little shakings of their heads, for the one thing that unites them at times is a youthful aversion to being tattle-tales—the one, recognized meanness and scheming disloyalty in their lives— and a desire to neutralize the obtuse interference which their parents are always making with the plans and goings-on of the children. At such times their differences become locked and partly forgotten behind closed mouths and sly looks, for then they change from three, disputing persons to Youth, waging the age-old battle against the prudences and self-comforting hagglings of Age—Youth, resolving to keep its purposes and impulses intact no matter how dreamless and contented it may be and regardless of whether these purposes concern nothing more than a good time at a dance, or a poker-game in a saloon, or a kiss from a boy met in the wood-shed and then instantly shelved. They have little hatreds and objections toward each other, these children, but they want to fight it out among themselves without what they consider to be the bungling, checking, over-talkative supervision of older people.*]

ALBRECHT. Well, what is it, what is it? You all

lost your tongues all of a sudden? You was talking about Elsie, wasn't you?

[*Not knowing just how much their father has heard, they are afraid to say no.*]

JOHN. Uh-huh, that's right.

ALBRECHT. Well, what was you saying? What was it?

ELSA [*compromising on a half-lie*]. Oh, they was pitching into me 'cause I ses I want to go to the dance to-night and they ses a girl gets flighty if she goes out too soon.

ALBRECHT. So, so, you could go if you go with your brothers, sure, you could go, but you got to be home by eleven o'clock on the dot. On . . . the . . . dot.

ELSA. Aw, I don't want to go to the old dance nohow. I'll wait till I'm old 'nough to go out with a fella, pa.

[ALBRECHT *squints at her with the facial cast of a charitable magistrate.*]

ALBRECHT. Yah, when you are seventeen I'll let you go out with boys, I'll let you, but chust remember, they got to be interdooced to ma and me first and we got to be sure they're good, decent boys.

ELSA. A-all right, pa, it's all the same to me.

．　　．　　．　　．　　．　　．　　．

Elsa was keeping rendezvous with a boy who worked in an adjacent ice-cream parlor—in the afternoon when a girl-friend called "to take her to my house"—and so, "let them talk for all the good it did them." He'd even kissed her, too, and she wasn't a bit ashamed of it. . . .

And now, the stenographer has dropped his pencil, having reproduced the exact words that the prototypes of his men and women would have uttered, with few omissions. A trivial achievement, but one worshiped by the "critics" of our country and time, who read into it a soil-steeped, salty projection of character and a thorough portrayal of those odds and ends that clutter up human motive and execution, and a difficult capture of indispensable local-color.

The afternoon was sunny and breeze-tickled as John hawked peanuts in the grandstand of the ball park and looked around for Elizabeth. The game was a close one between the White Sox and the Yankees, and John found it quite a problem to sell his wares and still peek at the more decisive plays going on in the field, for the temptation was to stand and take in the game and let the peanuts go hang themselves. His voice was cracking beneath the endless bawlings: "Fr-re-esh r-ro-oasted pe-eanu-uts, gents, fi-ive a copy. Get them while they're hot. Fr-re-esh r-ro-oasted pe-eanu-uts, boys, five a bag," and sweat was making his shirt stick to chest and back, and he had not yet acquired the art of always catching the coins tossed to him by men sitting in the middle, or end, of a seat-row, but these irkings were little more than gnat-stings swallowed up by the dramatic buzzings and roarings around him, and the thrill of turning to watch a fast double-play, or strike-out with the bases filled, or a whistling two-bagger to the right-field bleachers.

His menial position was made more relishing by the spirit of holiday and robust contest so close to him, and he felt less like a buffeted, unheeded boy forced to wait on his elders, less like an obscure oaf compelled to hurry through a small task because he lacked the talent to do anything better. Then again, the unseen proximity of Elizabeth made shrunken rainbows play tag in his head, and gave him the chimings and assonances attached to a feeling of vast sexual prowess, and lightened his work with the knowledge that he would soon be walking away with a different, real-honest, romantically met, good-to-look-at girl, who claimed to care for him. His sexual dream-and-seeking, prematurely rapped and vinegared by Mary Spielman and left much in abeyance by subsequent girls, was rallying itself in a second fight for life and using Elizabeth to serve as the illusion of a goddess—a girl standing apart from the prudes, flirts, and baggages of her sex, and one who could be treated frankly and yet bowed down to. . . .

Tragically valiant, fire-veined, beaten-ere-you-start Youth—they give you sex in a bundled maze of petticoats; garters just peeping out, brassières worn to keep the breasts from bobbing a little with the walking of legs; skirts to the ankles or stopping an inch above the knees; trousers that are creased sacks void of individuality; pulpit-lies and sacrosanct rantings; night-club shrieks and cavortings for coins (par-

don me, good-fellowship); newspaper heightenings
and moral melodramatizings; penny-arcades showing
women pictured in chemises, or less, and undisturbed
by envenomed censors; writhings, belchings, peepings,
philippics, traffickings, sweet denials, Mann Acts, eye-
winkings, harangues for chastity . . . anything, oh
anything but the clean extremes of rollicking, unpur-
chased, bold-minded nakedness, or contemplative
asceticism. And yet, you try to fight your way through
this clogged, cross-purposed, pettily striated skin-
game . . . hunt sometimes for a timorous, ignorant-
tongued beauty . . . chase the will-o'-the-wisp of
romance, which is nothing more than a ghost of hope
forever released from each death, each betrayal of
emotion . . . laugh at fulminating preachers and in-
sinuating wisecrackers alike. . . .

A roar swept the grandstand and John turned to
look at the field. It was the ninth inning and the
White Sox were three runs behind—the score was four
to one. The starting White Sox pitcher had been
driven out of the box after yielding three runs and the
game had been developed into a pitching-duel between
the relieving Sox flinger and the Yankee hurler, who
had a fast ball that struck the catcher's mit with a
rifle-report sound and a curve that became freakishly
incensed before it reached the plate and was liable to
drop, or rise, in any direction, almost as though the
ball had been personified. The second Sox pitcher,
however, had a slow ball that floated up to the plate,
like a little balloon just cleaving the air, and made the

batters strike at it a second before its arrival, and a
fast one without the necromancer-zip of its rival but
a round express-train nevertheless. The second Sox
pitcher had been scored on once in the fifth inning—
an error, a passed ball, and a stolen base sending the
runner to third, where he had gone home on a long
sacrifice-fly—but outside of this gift from his team-
mates he had not allowed a single other Yankee player
to get as far as second base.

Now the Sox were up in the last half of the ninth—
their final chance—and the crowd was booming,
stamping, hand-clapping, with cries rising above the
tumult—"Come on, Ed, a nice, little bingle," "Get
after him, boys, he's got nothing but his glove," "Come
on, you Sox, send that big bum to the showers," "Lean
on the apple, lean on it," "Make him pitch, Ed—let
the bad ones go," "Here's where we start—lam it out,
Eddie ol' boy." Peanuts be damned—John lowered
his half empty basket and watched the crisis on the
field. The gray uniforms of the Yankees, and the
soiled, white ones of the Sox, and the green of grass
and dull brown of ground around the bases, made a
color-scheme that was neither gaudy nor drab but sug-
gested shades of earth in an unmalicious and yet un-
sparing contention.

A last-minute baseball rally is an inexplicable out-
burst, with subconscious, or mystic, processes and ven-
tures operating beneath, or beyond, the romping of
limbs and torsos. If the rally is successful, it is cus-
tomary for sporting writers to say that the pitcher

weakened, when in reality his pitching changed not an iota and his strength was unimpaired. The change occurs in the batters, who have been popping up, hitting easy grounders, and striking out for eight innings. When they rally in the ninth and win the game, their ability at coördinating eyes and arms remains the same—it could not have been suppressed for any logical reason during eight innings and abruptly exercised in the ninth, unless they had been dishonestly withholding it—and their intelligence is not improved from any apparent cause, and yet they triumph over a pitcher whose throwing and brain also remain as they were. What is the answer? An unknown demon possesses them, from the bottom-pit of their hearts, with a *yes* to which flesh is but an obstructing putty. When they fail, this soul-signal (for want of a better word) does not rise and the batters continue to exert their natural skill and effort against a pitcher whose power stays in command. If we knew the reason for this unpredictable summons, or refusal, we might unlock the conundrum of a universe! Of course, in most cases the pitcher *does* weaken, thus causing the volley of hits, but not in *all*. . . .

The first Sox batter dropped a little bunt down the third-base line—a tauntingly modest one just beyond the reach of pitcher and third-baseman—and beat the ball to first by the tremor of an eyelash, as he slid feet first into the bag. The crowd yawped and veered near to delirium now, as it beheld this first, concrete carrying-out of that which had previously been but a yelling,

tottering hope. The second batter took two strikes and
three balls and then, at the moment of determining
tension, lifted a Texas Leaguer—a ball that dropped
between the running first baseman and right fielder
and barely eluded the latter, who tried to make a shoe-
string catch as he hurtled forward. Two men on bases
and no outs! The crowd was now in a vortex of ap-
peals and exhortations as men forgot their coin-grub-
bings, clothes-furbishings, and dollar-wearinesses, and
women deserted their lipsticks, protective modesties,
and mote-counting self-consciousness. These people
were starved for suspense, for fair, unmercenary com-
petition, unmercenary to the crowd at least, most of
whom had wagered nothing on the game: and for an
imagination-prodding uncertainty, and the death of this
starvation now yanked out their clearer selves—the
selves that were sidetracked, decried, grayed-over, and
polluted in offices, stores, boudoirs, and drawing-
rooms.

A fat, beribboned, ultra-respectable matron near
John had crossed her legs, with red garters showing in
fugitive flashings, and was twirling a score-card above
her head as she piped: "Beat the Yankees! Beat them,
boys!" . . . The next man up raised a fly caught by
the Yanks' left fielder, and the howling of the crowd,
which had increased until the catch was made—a
prayer that the fielder might drop the ball—now less-
ened to half of its former intensity, but slowly rose
again as the next batter came up. Two balls and no
strikes. One strike. Three balls. "Atta boy—make

'em be good!" . . . As he slowly raises his arms in the wind-up, the pitcher seems as cool as an animated cigar-store Indian, though inwardly he is having his share of snarling, confident, saturnine, moribund emotions. If these emotions can keep from seething over into each other, and can retain a succession in which the confident ones come *last*, his condition will continue to be unrattled. . . . Ball Four—he walked him! The ball was really a strike miscalled by the umpire, and the pitcher surveys him with a you-damn-fool look while the Yanks' manager runs in to protest, but the umpire waves him back. If the decision had been against the Sox batter the crowd would have screamed profanities at the umpire—civilization, your varnish is scarcely a fraction-of-an-inch coating!—but now it gloats and baits the Yankee manager as its yells swell up again. Three on bases and only one out!

The crowd becomes lost in an orgy of tossings, supplications, and abuse for the rival team. . . . One ball. One strike. Two balls, and then a high foul caught near the wire-screen behind the plate. With two outs now and only one more needed to end the game, the crowd senses the possibility of impending failure, and one-half of it ceases to yell while the other half redoubles its gyrations and bellowings—the old division between resilient faith and an easily drowned, realistic spirit that brightens up only when the tide seems to be swinging in its favor.

The next batter comes up, pulling the peak of his cap over his forehead, swinging his club to and fro to ease the boiling of his nerves, chewing gum with the precision of a motor, to keep all of his spirit on edge and in motion. . . . Ball one. Strike one. Strike two—a fierce swing at the ball. . . . Cr-ra-a-ack! The crowd is on its feet, gripped by a pandemonium. The ball flies in a low line to the screen in front of the left-field bleachers and bounces back, but the fielder fails to snare it on this rebound and is forced to pursue it as it rolls along the ground. Three men have raced home and the hitter—an unusually fast runner—is rounding third base. Contending cries: "Go on home," "Go on, you can make it," "Hold him back," "Stop him." . . . The ball is flying toward the third-base man and the coacher waves the runner back to third.

The game is tied now, four to four, with the winning run on third base. With the game now definitely removed from the imminence of loss, and with the home team's aroused, eleventh-hour power delightfully established, the crowd drops much of its frenzy, though it still cheers and gesticulates. No matter what happens now, an extra-inning game is assured at the worst. The best seems almost too good to hope for, with only one real hit made off the pitcher during the present inning-half and with two men already out. The next batter takes his stand at the plate and the crowd whoops and rampages again, with an undercurrent of expectation gone now, for the batter is the Sox pitcher —a weak hitter like most of his tribe. Some men in the crowd cry out for a pinch-hitter while others yell encouragement to the pitcher.

Strike One. Strike Two. Despairing pleas: "Come on, win your own game, Nick," "Give 'em a big surprise, Nick, ol' boy." And then, an unexpected anticlimax—a passed ball to the left of the catcher, who makes a flesh-wrenching stab at it! The runner sprints over the plate, a foot ahead of the returning catcher, and the crowd emits a last scream, almost perfunctory now, for this undramatic ending takes some of the punch out of victory. Five to four in favor of the White Sox. The crowd swarms over the field and jams up the aisles in the stands. A magic, unifying, breathless, dross-destroying touch has gone from the crowd and it splits up once more into thousands of men and women, each one hugging his slight variances in greed, and lust, and dissimulation, and ignorance, and social position, and sexual immediacies. . . .

John, who had been carried out of himself by the events on the field, returned to a reality compounded of forbidding and encouraging elements. Thank God this was over—shirt plastered to his back; voice sore and husky; arms tired from throwing bags of peanuts —the bags were light but the incessant motion exacted its toll nevertheless. He had arranged to meet Elizabeth in front of the box-seat turnstiles and he hurried below the stand to doff his white coat and cap, turn over his basket, and receive his pay. She had been signaling to him from a back seat in the grandstand but he had failed to spy her in the sea of moving faces. Perhaps she hadn't been able to come—now wasn't that like him, always hollering before he was hit? . . .

Nope, there she was, standing by one of the ticket booths and waving a hand to attract his attention. Wearing a long, starched, frilly, red and white muslin dress with a white leather belt at the waist, and a hugely round, high-crowned straw hat with plums and grapes on it—looked like a girlish, frisky, sparkling, unhurt wood-sprite masquerading as a human being but betraying itself in a slimness of body and a dainty quickness of limbs (his thoughts, with their fumblings rewarded by the preceding description, and not the impression that the author would have had on beholding a girl of Elizabeth's kind and outfit).

"Jo-ohn, didn't you see me waving to you all the time?"

"I sure didn't and I was looking all over for you, too."

"Why, you silly, blind boy, I almost waved my *arm* off."

"Guess I need a pair of specs. . . . Say, wasn't it a slam-bang game?"

"You bet it was. I thought I'd di-i-ie when they started going in that ninth inning. Why, d'you know, I dropped my hat and somebody almost stepped on it!"

They laughed and he felt just tickled to death with her, himself, and living. They rode in a carry-all to the Loop and sat in the balcony of a vaudeville theater and held hands and stroked each other's cheeks in the semi-darkness and compared notes on the clog-dancers and the possibility of emulating their rappy-

tarrapy jerkings and laughed at a song that went:
"Ah miss him in the mawning and ah miss him when
it's noon. No matter how we got along, ah always
miss dat coon. Ah miss him when he's flush and
when he never leaves a dime. Ah'm always *throw-
ing* at dat man but ah mi-i-iss hi-im a-all the ti-i-me!"
They had supper on a sandwich, a cup of coffee, and
a truly devouring smile (the only platitude that's right
is the one about love and eating!), and walked down
to Grant Park on the Lake Front and got cindery and
tindery and cream-puffy and short-winded as they made
love on a bench above the Illinois Central railroad
tracks, and were raped by reality at times when tramps
stopped to stare at them, or when one of a group of
girls passing by called out: "Aw, why don't cha hire
a room?" and would have sold their souls for the privi-
lege of not going home that night—a tabulation of the
curlicues and stencilings of emotion and action in-
dulged in by youth in such a situation would take
untold pages—all the little things which are prosy
spindrift to other people but which youth fondles and
inflames to an enormous stature and meaning.

As they rode back on the street car, Elizabeth
frowned suddenly and removed her arm from his, and
stared out of the window as though she had been
griped without warning and was averting her face to
prevent him from knowing it. He looked askance for
a moment and then thought that she had lit upon some
unpleasant thing in her personal life, which she would
tell him about later on. He tried to pull her forearm

toward him after a few minutes had gone, and when
she resisted him he woke up with a start—why this
mystifying coldness all at once? What had he done?
Girls were certainly tissue-papery, unplumbed creatures
(touchy and balky in his words)—you never knew
when they were going to fly up over next to nothing.

"What's the matter now? Why are you sore at me?"

"I'm not sore at you."

"Then what is it?"

Silence.

"Oh, all right, keep it to yourself then."

More silence.

"I wish you'd spout it out 'stead of leaving me in
the dark!"

"Oh, it's nothing, nothing, honest. I've got a blue
fit just now but I'll get over it, really I will."

He gripped her hand and felt restored and solicitous
—some uproar in her family, no doubt. Families were
like watch-dogs, sniffing and growling whenever some
new person came on the scene. If his own family knew
that he was growing slushy over her, they'd ask a thou-
sand questions and slip out a hundred don'ts, and
snoop around—nothing new and big happening in *their*
lives so they wanted to bag interest by bossing the
new ones in yours. He wouldn't ask her about it now
—he himself had spells when he hated to talk, couldn't
talk because he felt too heavy to dig for the right
words, or because he wasn't sure of what he wanted
to do.

She had been on the verge of revealing something

and then parting with him forever—forever, the poignantly bandied, fraudulently harsh, meant-at-the-time but afterwards relinquished, or regretted word of youth!—but tug and shove as she would, she had been unable to force the words from her lumpy, bludgeoned heart, much less from her mouth. The growing, stark and yet pellucid wrapping of word and touch wrought by this hook-nosed, near-swarthy boy, with his spearings, and effusive glees, and forthright questions, and prodigious, inept crusades for right things that most people didn't believe in, was too fetching and previously undreamt-of to be given up, no matter what might happen and in spite of the "terrible" impossibility that knocked the wind out of her. She had forgotten about the thing when she had first bumped into him, for the afternoon had been too amazing and too preoccupied with tilts against candor, boyish and girlish wrangles over decorum and what was "decent," confessions squeezed from her against part of her will, mock-strugglings against the sweet drugging of his kisses and hugs, and the eventual breakdown. Afterwards it had returned to her, puffed-up and blackened by the stage-craft of her youth, which favored extremes of nerve-bliss and staggering evacuation. Then, when she met him at the ball park, the abrupt wine of seeing him again, and the fidgeting softness of words and hand-pressures, had made her forget once more—the shiftings of youth often need a microscope and speedometer combined!—until, in the glaring, jarring street car, the thing had stormed her.

She was a negress—seven-eights white and one-eighth negro. Her great-grandmother in the south had borne a child to a white master and this child, Elizabeth's grandfather, had consorted with a white woman. This woman had given birth to a boy and the boy had married a white girl, whose daughter was Elizabeth. . . .

If negroes ever gain control of this earth, it will be a humorous retribution if they ostracize, flout, and penalize all people with an eighth, or sixteenth, of white blood in them, and if they fear that in some succeeding generation the offspring of these people may produce an all-white child. . . . Racial prejudice is a penetrating, corrosive, under-ground influence shared in some measure by almost all humans, from the profanely contemptuous lowbrow "up" to the most fairly protesting of artists and cultured acolytes. The ignorance of the lowbrow heaves in perfect conjunction with his purely physical recoiling—negroes are inferiors; they have a bad smell, particularly in the summer-time; they long to ravish white women; they are innate thieves and loafers; and they abuse any concessions made to them—ignorance uttering wild allegations to excuse a sensual withdrawal, but those cultured people, who desire to "keep negroes in their place" and restrict them from socially mingling with the white race, are plagued with vacillations and must try to rationalize their animal shrinkings. They would allow the negro to vote and acquire an education and creature-comforts but they insist that his flesh must remain apart from that of white people and that he should stick to his own theaters, cafés, and living-rooms. Obvious contrast of nudeness and draperies, yes, but the matter does not end here.

A third class has sprung into being—"emancipated" artists, writers, society people, professional men and women, who invite negroes to their parties; drink and eat with them; sit in cabarets and dance with them; attend banquets given by Associations for the Improvement of Relations between the Negro and White Races and utter kind words about Negro Art and fair-probing, serenely logical solutions of problems between the two races; and devote themselves to a study of the negro's intangible situation. Beautiful—the smashing-down of century-old barriers, hatreds, and clannish trappings . . . ah, if it only were! This creaking, massively-bound world of ours lumbers on a quarter-of-an-inch every thousand years—an optimistic opinion indeed—but during the course of these years it makes many misleading parades and declaimings of under-standing, prejudice-destruction, and brotherly love—a sporadic doping which any world-war can blast to smithereens. These nobly-talking, gayly-mixing people in the present third class never marry negroes and raise families with them; never have physical contacts with them unless alcohol takes the squeamishness out of white lust; never really sleep and live with negroes and reveal to them the deepest, barest, and most un-affected intimacies of heart and soul; never grab a pick, or a longshoreman's truck, and strain muscles

with them down in the sticky, ruthless dirt of life, to
find out what they are really thinking and feeling;
never actually intertwine breath, and skin, and heart-
beats with them. A stream of tolerant, serious, lofty,
praising, genial, sympathetic words—words not paid
for with raw chunks of heart and flesh; white speakers
in Tuxedo suits awarding fifty-dollar prizes to negro
poets and prosodists, before hand-picked audiences of
negroes and whites (the most experimental negro
creators are shunted off with honorable mentions, of
course); kisses and hugs in the gin- and whisky-soaked
flamboyancies of some white dilettante's home; negro
celebrities invited to white soirées; oh, yes, every facile
demonstration of good-will, social equality, and appre-
ciation, but scarcely a trace of heart-felt action, hum-
bly assiduous sincerity, and bottom-intermingling, to
buttress this lovely show, this flow of sound and social
amenities.   To understand a being one must walk
shoulder to shoulder with him and find lodging with
him, in every respect, since the bystander—however
much he may masquerade to himself and others—will
always lack those clues which reside only in eager and
never-flagging proximity. . . .

Unlike many of his kind—stupid, inwardly forlorn
outcasts, who claim to be entirely white to attain their
idea of social elevation and to protect themselves ma-
terially—Elizabeth's father, Joe Harrison, was proud
of the negro-fraction in his blood—a pride which he
used to lend dignity and size to his otherwise staidly
hollow, busily minor life—and he often made remarks

such as: "Ah'm a negro in mah heart even if the rest of me *is* white, and ah'm on the cuhllud man's side every time. The negro race has fought its way up from the ju-ungles, yes, suh, and it'll go a dahn sight highah befoh it's through." He would wax oratorical on this subject to white men of the neighborhood and some of them scowled at his nerve while others felt that they must be indulgent as long as he and his family kept to themselves. His white wife, Eleanor, bore the brunt of the neighbors' dislike, for in their opinion she should have been horse-whipped for marrying a negro and disgracing her race and bringing impure children into the world, but middle-class whites are slow to act when only one negro family lives in their midst—instead of an invasion—and when the objects of their dormant enmity show quiet habits and observe all of the decencies, church-going virtues, and regularities of their vicinity. The Harrisons had lived in Roseland for six years now and were accepted as "niggers" who, at least, didn't put on any airs and who made no effort to intrude upon the homes of their neighbors. They mingled only with relatives in the city and a few negroes largely of their own admixture of white and black blood, and Elizabeth had never gone out with a white boy. Boys of the neighborhood never disturbed her sister, Amy, whose physical immaturity was greater than that of the usual fifteen-year-old, but they had often tried to make secret dates with Elizabeth while she was going to the Roseland High School and afterwards.

Her parents had tried to instill in her the idea that white men would only seek her company "to ruin her" —negroes and whites who marry often become as conservative in their own way as the conservatism from which they once sought to escape!—and that she must loyally hang on to her own kind—not full-blooded negroes necessarily, but those who had at least a dash of Ethiopian in them. Instinctively her heart had bled and cried out against this proscription—her parents certainly hadn't lived up to it, or she'd never have been born, and if she should ever love a boy she wouldn't care whether he was white, pink, or purple—but without an emotional incentive to disobey them in the form of a white boy sharply attractive to her, and with her sexual desires still pulsing embryos, she had moodily followed her parents' instructions.

Now, as she sat beside John in the jolting street car, a veritable little fanfare of emotions was in her heart— one that would defy prose and needed the impish-stern, spartanlike struggle against snores, psalms, and snickerings, which is one kind of poetry . . .

She found a negro baby in a sewer
And kissed the offal from its head and chest,
And with each kiss the child became less brown
And more the bloom-breath dream of pink and cream,
Too thick to be a vapor but not quite
The bundling flexibility of skin.
A saturation of nightmarish brown
Had robbed the baby of reality,

And when she kissed it off, the skin remained
Untingling and immune to pain and joy.
One speck of dung stayed on the baby's head.
She kissed it till her breath shrank to a wisp
Of scarcely moving life, but still the speck
Clung to the baby's head, like some horsefly
Perched on the head of beauty not yet born
Because one small objection would not die.
Then hatred plumbed her with its gutturals.
Her fingers tore the speck and then her teeth
Sank into it, while frenzied loathing gave
Her soul the false guise of a tiger-bitch
Half William Blake, half dankest jungle-spawn.
The brown spot stayed: she slipped upon her knees
And watched it with an unbelieving, whipped,
Exhausted light faint on her jerking face.
A mirror dropped from nowhere and she saw
The same spot clinging to her own small head.
A premonition of eternity
Could not have been more fixed, more dominant.
She touched it with her fingers and it seemed
The clue to all her loves and enmities,
The mingling pride and fear that made her stand
Precariously balanced on the line
Where laughs and weepings change identities.
Would she stand thus until the end of life,
Never completely happy, deeply sad,
But caught between a wound and healing smiles?
The answer seemed to be a yes and no
That mocked her, like a figure tossed by time

And never standing still to be discerned.
She tried to love this brown spot and to feel
Unique and consecrated loneliness
Within a world of men and women tinged
Unbrokenly—the effort failed because
Self-pity and repugnance left their ghosts
To loiter in dark lulls between her prides.
Her mother came, a worn-out woman made
Of resignations, fancies shrunk to rows
Of kitchen-pans, and memories of lust
Faint red on babbling duties, and she asked
Her mother, with compassion in her voice:
"Why did you swell this brown spot into life?"
Her mother frowned and pointed to her breast
And said: "Love is the dream-large death of fear—
The time in which we look not to the left
Or right, but walk straight to our destiny
And smile alike at Hell and Paradise!"
The girl grew still with understanding wrought
Of slicing knives between great gulps of wine.
A white boy came—he could not see the spot
Upon her head and asked her why she wept,
And when she told him, darkness clapped its hands
And she was left alone, cold-naked, bruised,
Within a void where minutes were as dead
As pebbles rattling on her metal breasts. . . .

It must be remembered that this poem represents
Elizabeth's feelings and is not one that the author
would have written in the rôle of a complete bystander

to Elizabeth, since objective and subjective dictates
can often bow to each other's requirements. . . . When
the car was nearing Ninety-third Street, Elizabeth
sighed as though the seat had just returned to her
back, and said: "Johnny, dear, please don't see me
home to-night. You get off at Ninety-third and let
me ride along, please, dear."

This request shook him out of his tender, silent faith
—what in hell had happened to her ever since they
took the car? Pulling her arm away, hiding her face,
refusing to talk, and *now*, asking him not to take her
to her house. Something was wrong and he'd find out
mighty quick.

"Say, what's all this? Why can't I see you home,
huh? Ever since we got on this car you've been acting
like ten below zero, and I want to know what it's all
about."

His snapping voice and the cuffed look on his face
gave her a criminal, pitying, tight-lipped feeling—she
was hurting him badly and she'd have to lie, oh, ever
so skillfully, since she couldn't tell him the truth in
such a scene and time as the present one and didn't
even know whether she wanted to tell him.

"It's this way, Johnny—my parents are awf'lly,
awf'lly strict with me and I just know my father's
sitting out on the front porch now and waiting for me
to show up. I just know it. You see, I couldn't tell
them who you was 'cause they'd have asked me all sorts
of questions 'bout how I met you and, oh, everything,
so I told a whopper of a lie and I said I was going out

with another boy. Please, Johnny, don't see me home,
e-eve-er, till I tell ma and pa all about you . . .
please."

Her words were deliciously plausible, and his sus-
picions had had no tangible basis, and the explanation
was exactly what he had wanted to hear, and he had
all of the trumpet-following, plunging-in, semi-dense,
glimmering seethings of youth, whose glowering dis-
trusts and huge beliefs need scarcely the shadow of a
shove to make them turn tail. He gave her a quick,
self-conscious kiss and wringing of hands, and then
jumped from the still-moving car, with a hosanna
rounding out his heart. . . .

The next four weeks did much to change him from
a boy to the beginning of a man—from a raring, blood-
ripping, do-it-to-morrow kid to a screwed-up, wonder-
ing, planning-ahead man. A first love does that to a
boy of his kind, whose untold dreamings have been
quartered in the parlor-camouflaged latrine of a few
other people's fears and misinformations—with few
words to bring them an expanding edge, these dream-
ings seize upon the first pretext for strong emotion, to
break down the latrine-doors and gamble and ramble
within an outside world. Being in his fundamental
texture neither a poet, nor an artist, nor an elemental
laborer, nor a middle-class being of normal conceal-
ments and heart-auctions, nor a wastrel, nor a physi-
cally insane imaginer, and yet holding portions of all
these conditions shifting and momentarily merging in

his make-up, John belonged to the almost-class of human beings—intermediates whose qualities are so dangerously and lightly arranged and crossed that they are entirely at the mercy of chance, with any stray smile, curse, or tear, from another, able to turn them into murderers, samaritans, peaceful citizens, vagabonds . . . but never permanently and always open to what might be called key-events—happenings exactly fitted to turn these people upside-down once more . . . to-morrow, next month, ten years from the present. If they are lucky, they become second-rate talents and live their span with only secondary upsettings and invasions. Second-rate—who knows? It is possible that in the cosmical scheme, whose methods and purposes can only be guessed, John Musselman looms as large as Baudelaire, Buddha, Villon. We have invented the word genius to crown, hushedly interview, and immortalize the objects of our most meticulously sheltered and objective loves and mental seclusions, and another word, æsthetics, to extract and elevate effortlessly appropriate patterns in the more common jumble that greets our senses, and another word, intelligence, to admire and standardize the centering of initiatives and informations most in harmony with that within our own minds, but few words have any unassailable, indispensable meaning except nouns of earthly plainness, such as house, wall, hill, pond, road; steadily recurrent adjectives—blue, red, bitter, large, surly, small, happy, uncertain; and their shading adverbs. The rest are experiments with thought and emotion; encrustations

left by decrepit faith and dogma; backwash of former
adventures now turned to prudences; thought adjust-
ing itself to the violence or gentleness of emotion; and
haloes and blunderbusses made by the surface of
egotism. . . .

John met Elizabeth three and four times a week dur-
ing the month following his first Sunday with her, but
these sessions will not be etched, or amplified. John
and Elizabeth enrolled in a dancing- and vocal-school
in the Loop—a suite of offices on one of the top floors
of a skyscraper, where over-strident, uninspired, rose-
moire singers, tap-dancers just fit for five-a-day vaude-
ville, toe-dancers of bare competence, and "interpre-
tive" hoppers were ground out with the regularity of a
threshing-machine. The proprietor of the school,
Signor Carlo Di Alberti—who had won medals in Rome
that no one had ever beheld and who had a golden-
framed diploma from the Roman Conservatory of
Music and Dancing hanging on his office wall (whether
the Conservatory was fictitious, or existent, scarcely
mattered in its relation to Di Alberti's essence and
methods)—was a short man of thirty-five, with a little
torrent of black hair, and a face where a gargoyle
and angel had decided to laugh at each other and used
the large twist of a nose, the smallest of bow-shaped
lips, dimples in the fattest of cheeks, and the debacle
of a chin, to solidify their humorous objections! He
had toured the sticks and the cheapest of vaude-
ville houses in "Scenes from Famous Italian Operas,"
and he knew a smattering of ballet-dancing, and he

could bluff, intone, and twirl his wrists in a manner that made even dancers and singers of minor ability believe that "he knew something," and that, in spite of his excitable and cerise-dapper personality, he could qualify as a moderately grounded supervisor of the twin arts with which his school dealt.

Elizabeth looked on him as a great, accomplished man of the world and felt sure that she could become a great singer under his guidance, for winking an eye to himself he had "a-ahed" and trilled and gurgled over her thinly sweet, limited, soprano voice. 'Yes, yes, he was captivated by the signorina's tone and range, but she might have to study for several years at his school—voice de-vel-op-*me-ent* took oh wo-orlds of patience and time, and, of course, the signorina would not wish to study a year or so just for some trifling vaudeville-booking . . . nothing but Grand Opera would suit the timbre and richness of her voice!' This was Di Alberti's line until he saw that the pupil was not bowled over, or could not raise the money for extended tuition, in which case he gave him a few months of rudimentary, humdrum instruction and sent him out to warm the chairs of the lowest theatrical agencies in Chicago and all points east. If the pupil really had an exceptional voice, Di Alberti tried to hang on to him and make him a fifty-a-week teacher in the school, or to induce him to sign a contract in which he would agree to give up one-third of his earnings in return for an extra-singer's job in Opera, or a small part in some musical comedy.

Elizabeth saw herself working for years to pay for three nights a week at his school, but she did not blanch at the prospect—she was the anomaly of a morbidly intense plodder: a girl who was ruffled and spent inside but had an outer reserve force that never lost the steadiness of its beat. John paid little attention to Di Alberti except to consider him a namby-pamby, scented, cooing joke of a man—he was too grimly crated in his lessons and his quarrelings and making-up with Elizabeth to notice a "twittering" monkey, who might be efficient as a singer and dancer but was a disgusting mite otherwise. His quarrels with Elizabeth were caused by her refusal to let him visit her at her house, or accompany her there, and by the fuss she made over Di Alberti. This sneaking 'round on the outside had been an inviting, romance-plastered, dodging-for-love plot at first, but now it began to seem shabbily skulky and suspiciously mysterious—it could not go on forever and she'd have to let her parents know some time, and he didn't want to feel like a coward unwilling to face their wrath. Go straight up to them and tell them: "Sure, I'm going with 'Lizabeth and I want to be friends with you, see? You're not bears and you won't bite me, I guess." If he hadn't meant to hang on to her he would have welcomed this avoidance and secrecy as measures which would make it easy for him to break with her at any time, but she had driven the slangy, breezy, idling cruelties out of his heart and replaced them with an alternation of serenity, prickling delight, and anger, and he still "flew

up in the air" when he touched her, and her stumble
of thought was usually on a par with his. He couldn't
tell himself why he loved her—he, the budding women-
juggler who had meant to play with tens of girls!—
except to say that she was fine and honest and just a
load of bliss in his arms. . . .

Di Alberti scarcely ever meddled with the girls in
his school, since he shrank from the possibility of
policemen and investigation ruining his golden fraud,
and he satisfied himself with a "fatherly," accidental,
"impersonally" manipulated dropping of hands on
their knees and shoulders, standing close to their sides
while examining a sheet of music with them, and strok-
ing their arms a bit, but when he tried these tactics
on Elizabeth and she failed to shrink away, or walk
out of range, he started to eye her up as a possibility.
He grew a little bolder then, and pinched her arms and
patted her cheeks, and when she received these over-
tures passively he felt certain that he could possess her.
To his mind, a refined and practically inexperienced
girl never showed any active response to a man at first
but tacitly revealed her willingness by allowing him
to go further and further without objections, since such
a girl would not care to give a man the impression that
she was readily for sale and could be caught without
courtship, or some semblance of hesitant technique.

Bound with his two-inch worldly-wisdoms and shoddy
rules wrung from past experiences with over-sexed
ninnies, professional nymphomaniacs, and prudes who
could be slowly flattered into nudeness, he did not

realize that Elizabeth's passiveness under the tentative intrusions of his fingers was caused by an immersion in her work so great that these fingers gave her only the veriest of almost unheeded brushings. If he had sought to kiss her, or wind an arm around her waist, she would have waked with a start and ordered him to stop, but even when she remembered them afterwards they seemed to be no more than little, comradely, inoffensive contacts. Di Alberti knew that she always left the school with John and seemed to be attached to this boy but . . . she was probably hanging on to the conceited yokel only to mark time until *he*, Signor Di Alberti, made actual love to her. Di Alberti's own conceit would have made a balloon seem solid in comparison, and it often rendered negative the lessons brought by a life in which slights and rebuffs and seamy pits had not been absent.

One night, Elizabeth and John stood in the reception room of the school and quarreled with each other—the old subject of keeping away from her parents.

"To-morrow's Sunday, and I'm coming out to your house. Your folks can't eat me *alive,* and if they try to, well, then I'll go with you anyway no matter what they do, but I'm no criminal and I want to have it out with them."

"No, you mustn't, John. We've only known each other a month, and there's plenty of time."

"Oh, plenty of time be darned!"

"John, don't talk to me like that—I won't stand for it."

"Sit down to it then, I don't care. I've had enough of all this sneaking 'round the bush."

"Please don't call me a sneak. They don't want me to go out with any boys till I'm twenty; I've told you that a hundred times, and all you'd do would be to make it im-pos-si-ble for us to see each other. Is that what you want?"

"No, you know it isn't, but I'd rather have *that* than act like I was yellow! They couldn't stop us from meeting each other 'less they locked you in the minute you came back from work, and I know they wouldn't go that far."

"Oh, you know it, do you? Well, *I* don't."

She was sick to the core of her heart with all of the lying and fencing and half-real exasperation that she had to utter to keep him from finding out that she was a negress and to prevent her family from ordering her not to see him again, but she clung to these utterances because she couldn't decide on a more truthful course of action—couldn't give him up; shrank from his possible scorn, or departure, if he should discover what she was; found herself unable to see the smallest gleam of any solution; and cared only for procrastination, as a child might long to hide from the dark, or the spleen of its elders.

"All right, I'm through with you then . . . so long" —he turned and walked off with quick steps, and a whirling of snarls and hurt whispers in his heart.

He had abruptly walked away from her twice before, with almost the same words on his lips, and each time he had relented with inward groans because he couldn't stay away from the painless fires and dissolving swoons of physical contacts with her, and the tricks and slips and wispy inflections and shades within her voice and on her face, but all of this was unremembered now just as it had been the last time he had flung himself away from her. A maniac, a sentimentalist, and a whimpering stripling took him at the times when he could not budge her, and he would stride away then not entirely in anger but partly to hold himself back from beating her face, or winding his fingers around her throat. When he absolutely *knew* he was right, and when the other person, mattering greatly to him, persisted in stupidly (in his opinion) opposing this knowledge, then he felt unbearably frustrated and flogged and wanted literally to beat insight into her (or his) face and body, and was capable of committing murder itself without realizing the finality of such an act until it had been consummated, and swayed only by this craving to assail the human symbol of an obtuse injustice that would not retreat. His climactic angers against Elizabeth were but the youthful forerunners of others which were to lead him to the electric-chair. . . .

Before Elizabeth had time to adjust her emotions he slammed the door leading to the hall and elevators, and without reasoning she started to hurry after him, but checked herself suddenly, with a musing, unworried smile on her face. Oh, let him bustle off—he got rid of extra-steam that way and put on a great show of being

a rough, I'm-master man, and wanted to see whether
she'd come running after him—she *had* run after him
the last time but this time she'd surprise him. To-
morrow was Sunday, and in the afternoon he'd be sit-
ting under that tree where she'd first met him, just as
he had last Sunday after swearing that he'd never speak
to her again . . . sitting there and just *praying* that
she would have an instinct about where he was, and
turn up. If she was wrong . . . oh, well, though neither
one knew where the other lived, she'd run into him
at the school on the coming Tuesday and speak to him
first, if he was still grumpy. Yet, the sickness stole
back to her heart in spite of the girlishly gloating
realization that she had the upper hand—a spinning-in-
emptiness, confused, self-dwindling feeling. "Oh, how's
it going to end?" she asked herself. "I won't be able
to keep this up all the time."

Di Alberti had been leaning behind one of the opaque
glass doors that stood around the reception room and
listening to the unconsciously raised voices of Elizabeth
and John with a lip-smacking, penny-splitting species of
misunderstanding. Of course, this girl refused to let
the boy come to her home because she was ashamed
to introduce him to her people and didn't want them
to know that she was lowering herself by going around
with such a penniless simpleton, and because this was
a good way of leaving him without taking the first
step herself. Girls were like that—always making it
look as though they hadn't been responsible for *any-
thing* and were as innocent as doves . . . the feminine

slyness that every wise man knew about. Di Alberti's malicious astigmatisms pounced on the words he had heard, much as a Broadway newspaper columnist leaps upon slanderous visions and conjurings. And now she had let him walk off without chasing him, or saying another word—conclusive proof that all she had wanted was to get rid of the boy. Everything was lovely now.

He walked into the reception room just as Elizabeth was nearing the door to the outside hall.

"Oh, Mees Harreeson, just a mi-inute, eefa you please."

She turned as he approached her with a deferential and yet confident brother-to-a-smile on his face.

"I would appreciate little talk with you, uh, about your ca-areer. I have been thinking maybe I could give you free scholarship effa you are finding it, uh, deefi-cult to pay for your tuition."

"Why, gee, that would be wonderful"—her face had sparkles. "You know, I've been finding it very hard to raise the money for my lessons here, 'cause I don't earn much at all where I'm working now."

They stepped into his office and then he excused him-self—he wanted to hurry the remaining teachers off so that he could be alone with her. He returned in a few minutes, beaming and rubbing his fingers together, like a semi-humanized monkey planning a raid upon the cupboard. He dilated on the matter of the scholarship as he sat beside her and used words to postpone and toy with the delectable session waiting for him—he wanted gracefully to lead up to eventualities instead

of acting like a hard-up clod—women liked such pre-
liminary appetizers. When he pinched her cheek and
she did not lose her infant, eager smile—she was still
dizzy at her good fortune and attributed it to his faith
in the power and future of her voice—he felt that no
further sparrings were necessary.

He pulled her to her feet and kissed and hugged her
while he whispered love-phrases in Italian—fragments
of songs which he had taught her, so that she would
understand them and be irrevocably melted by their
"beauty." With the ending of her surprise, she
wrenched herself away in a business-like manner that
was too questioning to be contemptuous and too un-
moved to be irritated but drew near to both qualities.
Being neither a coquette nor a chastity-flaunter, she
had no reproaches or pretendedly offended oglings to
give him—she was concerned only with making it plain
that she didn't want him and with finding out whether
his scholarship offer had been dependent on her re-
sponding to him.

"I don't want you to kiss 'n' hug me 'cause I don't
like you that way. I'm really and truly in love with
somebody else, Mister Di Alberti, really and truly."

"You lova thata fool keed, Johnny?"

"Yes, I do love him very much, and don't you call
him a fool kid either. Maybe he *doesn't* know as much
as you, but you're a lot older than he is."

They looked at each other for a short while—in-
credulity, slashed vanity, and unvarnished lust play-
ing with his face: sober inspection and withdrawal on

hers. His feelings, jabbed and untied by his recent con-
tacts with her face and bosom, overcame the hidebound
judgments in his head, which told him that this girl
wouldn't be so frigidly removed now, when everything
was perfect and clear, unless she was sincere—no, no,
in spite of her present words she *must* be flipping him
on, or else she would never have allowed the previous
familiarities of his hands. Evidently, she was pitting
the boy against him to make him jealous, make him
fight hard for her—the kind that liked a huge struggle
before they gave in because it made them feel more
commanding and valuable.

He tried to hug and kiss her, drawing near to violence
this time, and she had a simple wrath at his disbelief
and insistence as she jerked away from him after a
half-minute of struggling that was practically a
wrestling-match.

"You keep your hands off me, d'you hear? I mean
e-eve-ery wo-ord of it, and I've got a good notion not
to come back here again. Why, I'll bet a nickel you
just talked about your old scholarship to see whether
I'd be nice to you—I know. You're a rotten, mean
wo-op, that's what you are!"

The word "wop" fell like a spark on his lust and
kindled it to a Latin fury—vanities immune to mean-
ingful insults and imputations of unscrupulous conduct
can often be split asunder by some epithet that ferrets
out the little sore spot in their robust immensity, and
Di Alberti's racial pride, though neither fine nor sacri-
ficing, was a furious verity nevertheless . . . insulting

brat . . . dirty liar of a puppy . . . nigger that she was, he'd wager his life on it . . . tear her to pieces . . . show her what a wo-op could do . . . crowded tornado in his heart, expelling all the furtive, oily, stalking discretions. He snatched a lead paper-weight from his desk. She ran toward the door but he overtook her and swung the weight against her head. She fell to the floor.

.   .   .   .

As Elizabeth walked down the Burnside railroad-tracks on the following afternoon, she felt a century of effort and uselessness in each step, motion seeming to her just going nowhere, nowhere, with a mean attack here, and a stone wall there, to make her detour and drag her feet in some other unprofitable direction. . . . Got a travelin' mind but ah got no railroad, said ah got no ra-ailro-oad fa-are—got fa-are—but if mah shoes hold out, swe-eet bo-oy, ah'm gointa meet you the-ere, ye-es the-ere. . . . Meet what? A bang on the head when they couldn't get you no other way; or the whole pack barking at you 'cause you loved a white boy; or nine hours of snipping at ribbons and pushing with needles in a shop; or staying at home too tired to stir your legs. A spiritual blazed up in her head, with its refrain: "Ho-ow d'you kno-ow that Je-esu-us lo-oves yo-ou? 'Cause he ki-issed mah fe-eet on the go-oldu-un stre-eet. Ho-ow d'you kno-ow that Je-esu-us lo-oves you? 'Cause he ki-issed mah fe-eet o-one da-a-ay." . . . She sure hoped that Jesus would punish the man who had done her wrong last night. But, gawd, wasn't no punishment fit for him.

Miserably enough, she thought of a favorite joke of her father's—Jesse James rapped on the red-hot, nine-miles-high gates of Hell and the Devil came out and stared at Jesse, and then the Devil threw his pitchfork down and started to walk off, and Jesse hollered: "Hey, there, where yuh goin'?" and the Devil turned and said: "After taking one look at *you,* I've decided I'm good enough for Heaven!" . . . Her religious side was kin to a lie but had never investigated itself sufficiently to produce any inner cataclysm. She had swallowed the tenets of the Baptist Church with a thoughtless spirit that threw them aside the moment she tripped out of the church-vestibule, and regarded them as true because they *did* sit in the hearts of her wiser parents and because most of the world believed in them (her opinion), and though she prayed to God sometimes in a girl-like, wondering-whether-to-hope, briskly singsong tumbling out of words, it was primarily a duty and a virtuous ratification to her. Religion—in the sense of believing in a soul patterned after those qualities considered to be purest and most kindly on earth, and a God, Christ, Buddha, or Mohammed with narrowly judging and castratedly human aspects, and some picturing of a restful, or benignly still Here-After—is a receptibility and seraphically mantled fear inherent in some people and completely lacking in others, no matter how temporarily buried it may be in the former, or earnestly professing in the latter, which is the reason why bank-robbers and Bowery tramps sometimes crash down to their knees at Mission meetings and become sincerely converted for the remainder of their lives, while sextons, small-fry workers, and millionaires attend church-services during an entire lifetime without believing, or even attempting to follow, the precepts which they hear and repeat . . . *a tot-like, really cleansing, fear-sublimated, ever-fresh conjuring, which many imitate but only a chosen few possess.* And thus religion—a passionate verity to a few children and a convenience, or thin delusion, to hosts of other humans, stands apart from the lip-serving worshipers, and the opposing wisecracking skeptics, who live in any generation. . . .

The afternoon was capriciously sunny, with a southwest breeze that curled up the green elephants'-ears, box-weeds, and nettles on the sides of the ditches along the tracks, but it was just a neutrally tinted void to Elizabeth. Although she caught the flowers, greeneries, and rails, as though they were refracted from a distant shore beyond the borders of the blank through which she was striding, she tried to make them substantial with the fixity of her eyes. Di Alberti's image—especially the last-remembered splintering of Ape-rage on his face, with strands of black hair over his eyes—vanished and reappeared spasmodically. What she felt toward him was not blood-hatred, and not the forgiveness that springs from an alliance between fear and self-depreciation, and not the skin-contused indignation that can forget a week later, but an indescrib-

able, never-still growth and interchange of emotions
—blisters on bits of misused blushing . . . angers
feeling themselves small against the impersonal,
trampling bulk of life . . . perplexity—oh, how could
sex be such a toad and bliss-load at different times
and still remain sex? . . . a feeling of flesh mistreated
by forces stronger than the hands of any man—why
was *she* picked out to be waylaid, when thousands of
girls went around unmolested to any serious extent,
oh, why? . . . a thrice-ashamed-of-itself but dimly-
surviving wonder whether she might not have missed
a sizable pleasure by passing into unconsciousness—
did any girl really *know* how she felt toward a man,
in that way, unless he overcame her, no matter how
terrible it might seem to be beforehand (instinctive
promptings of what the all-seeing world would call the
birth of a courtesan?—no indeed!)? . . . and a feel-
ing that Di Alberti was like most men except that he
had more conceit and absolutely no scruples. . . .
These sensations and musings and many others, ever
slipping, slipping into each other in the unrewarded
depths of her mind and heart.

She had come to her senses in a cab—Di Alberti had
forced a sleeping-powder down her mouth to prolong
her unconsciousness and had then sprinkled some
whisky on her face and clothes and persuaded the
night-porter, who ran the elevator after 11 p.m.,
to help him carry her out to a cab, with the explanation
that she had passed out because of drunkenness—a
liberal tip to the porter helped in this regard. . . .

Frightened, dazed by the throbbing lump on her head, and weakly summoning the driver to stop, she discovered that Di Alberti had paid him and given him her address and that she was rolling toward her home. She became silent then and slumped down in the cab and tried to force some practical looking-ahead into the numb instabilities within her brain. It was a little after one in the morning—the driver had told her the time—and her parents might be up and frenziedly waiting. . . . Luck was with her—they had gone soundly to sleep at ten without waking afterwards. Elizabeth's returning later than eleven, unless she was attending a dance, or theater, which happened seldom, was too unprecedented for them to consider in advance, and she had managed to stagger into the house without arousing them. . . . In the morning she had explained the lump on her head by fibbing about a fall on a stairway . . . endless fragments of lies uttered to prevent the frozen-dreamed, or hotly dreamless, honorable, claw-bearing, valiantly-justified-unto-itself, phrase-making, law-worshiping and yet law-breaking *busybodiness* of other people from intruding into another person's life with melodramatic revenges, harangues, tear-spotted beseechings, silent disapprovals —a world of people intent on doing everything except healing with sympathy, or else leaving each other in peace, when not directly solicited, and when physical injury and danger are no longer looming and can no longer be remedied. . . .

John had been waiting under the tree—nerve-

ticking; filled with tirades against the way he had of
stepping on his own heart; string-plucked by andantes
and pizzicatos of hope. When he saw her clambering
down the farther side of the ditch he ran forward—
head poised now, and with a little of the bending-down
prince pardoning an errant subject because he loved
her defects and misdeeds. These lightning-changes
from torn-apart, praying slavishness to high-handed
self-belief were ineradicable—symptoms of his uncen-
tralized nature. . . . After they had kissed, the varia-
tions differed little from those of previous meetings fol-
lowing quarrels—never a single word concerning the
past disagreement; acting as though they had never
deserted a singing closeness; talking at a furious rate
about dumbnesses and drolleries in the people whom
they knew, to forget their own "foolishness" of a few
hours previous; plans for the future; and embraces
that erased tree, grass, and waiting homes. Somehow
purged and remade by seeing him again and by his
happy compliances and faiths, Elizabeth almost forgot
about Di Alberti and the past wreck of a night, but
they came back when she remembered that she couldn't
return to the school now and that John mustn't know
the reason for her departure. If she told him, he might
try to kill Di Alberti, or fight with him, and then
everybody would find out and she would be talked
about, pitied, bawled-out, cross-examined, laughed-at
—u-ugh.

"I'm quitting the school, Johnny"—in a would-be
casual voice that shook a bit.

"You're *quitting?* What for?"

"Aw, I'm tired of that darn wop who runs it. I heard he wasn't so muchy-much of a teacher nohow and I don't think he's helping my voice one bit. 'Sides, I'm sick of the way he stands close to me when I'm singing —like he meant nothing, you know, oh, no-othing what-at-so-o-e-ever, but always eying me up just the same."

She used the words to imagine that the past night had not happened—vain imagining—and then to find a dark relief in cursorily pitching into Di Alberti without a confession, as though he had been powerless to injure her and should not be dwelt-upon, and John heard them with satisfaction.

"I don't blame you the least bit—if that slob's a lady-killer then I'm a hunk of cheese."

"You said something."

"I've got a good notion to take a swat at him for standing close to you."

"No, Johnny, please don't. I'm not going back again and he doesn't matter enough. Promise me you won't."

"All right, I won't then, but he's got it coming to him, the stuck-up wop."

Seconds of silence.

"I'm going to stay another two weeks, 'cause Blake says I'll be good enough to get a part in some show by then. Blake could murder a guy for two cents, yepee, and I wouldn't trust him 'round the corner, but he *is* a good tap-teacher and that's all I care about."

Relieved by his unquestioning response, she switched

the subject and made up her mind to treat the whole,
past night as a spine-broken nightmare . . . somehow
try to do it, for her own happiness as well as John's.
Di Alberti shouldn't have the power to ruin her entire
existence, and he wouldn't either, if she stiffened her
lips and threw off the whole memory of his rottenness.
Maybe she couldn't do it, but she'd certainly try her
darndest. . . . The sun was speckling a bunch of gray-
white clouds near the horizon when Elizabeth and
John walked off, with arms interlocked and tongues
still twirling the warmness of commonplaces that were
small carolings to the two speakers, and prophecies of
future success and freedom.

He met her again after supper, in front of a candy-
store near the Illinois Central suburban-train station
in Burnside, and they rode back to Roseland and went
to one of the little, moving-picture theaters just bud-
ding up at that time. The picture displayed—"The
Foreman of the Double-Bar Ranch"—was a western
dime-novel in which the usual aggregation of sloppy,
morally veneered, blood-curdling, hastily-dumped
words were supplanted and visualized by an hour of
photographed human beings, gyrating, lassoing, and
posturing. . . .

Moving-pictures of the present—even the finished,
compact, and fresher ones, which feature Emil Jan-
nings, John Gilbert, Lilian Gish, and others—have not
lost this essential focusing on melodramatic realism,
this centering on physical tussles and spun-out love-
scenes where kisses and embraces are lengthily fore-

shadowed, or delineated with interminable close-ups;
this feverish use of legs and arms to mold and hurry
bald versions of primary emotions; this immersion in
realistic plots whose deviously postponed endings can
be guessed in the middle of the first reel; this passion
for transparent "surprises" and lugged-in stunts—a
condemned murderer playing checkers with a guard
on the outside of his cell, in one flash, and then escap-
ing in the next through a ruse that any quick-witted
twelve-year-old could have circumvented; this seizure
of everyday life, in which it is squeezed and panoplied
to a half-sweet, half-hectic pretentiousness, attended by
thousands of faithful reportings of customs and col-
loquialisms, to lend an air of plausibility to the deeper
falseness of ideas and hurried emotions; this inadequate
suggestiveness striving to be complete realism, where
a business-man signs two or three papers to represent
his day's work, and a laborer swings his pick four
or five times to indicate his grueling toil, and a house-
wife dabs at a sinkful of dishes, for ten seconds, and
then hastens to her lover. In other words, the realistic
stage of our day, robbed of grease-paint and actual
flesh and shortened upon a white expanse. The acting
is much more adroit now; the plots are much more
clever and polished-up; the material ranges from sub-
marine and circus to tenement-houses and battle-
trenches; and the photography often uses novel and
expressionistic effects to further a more common and
unshaded content-matter, but essence and aim remain
the same as they were in "The Foreman of the Double-

Bar Ranch" beheld by Elizabeth and John years ago.

Poetry, with its braidings and flashings of feeling in-
terplaying beneath a quieter use of human legs and
arms; character-analyses, mind-dissectings, and heart-
shakings dominating an entire picture with subtle whiffs
of facial expression occurring over *motionless bodies;*
fantasies employing realistic symbols only to cut below
the exhausted reiterations of "reality" and substitute
fresher ideas and appearances (fantasy is never more
than reality in a more awakened and unbound condi-
tion!); ideas, void of propaganda and fixed solutions,
and caring only for the pure heat of discovery and
battle against obstructions within themselves; ten min-
utes in the lives of one, two, or three human beings,
expressed through the juxtaposition of microscope and
telescope; what transpires in the niches and pits of
human hearts and minds, beneath the interminable
round of eating, walking, coin-earning, dancing, flesh-
meeting, and physical contention; melodrama adopted
and adapted only to point at the more impersonal causes
behind its emerging (impersonal because they stand
beyond human beings and yet represent the sum-total
of life); ungushing sentimentalities and disapproving
thoughts in a clear-cut, honestly handled conflict
against each other—all of these potentialities are
largely absent from the moving-pictures of our day.

To John and Elizabeth "The Foreman of the Double-
Bar Ranch" was a blessing that shut off the more dis-
creet and confined incidents and observances within
their lives, and they cared not a whit about whether

it was true, or untrue, accepting the sheer relief of its
different scenes and people. John felt that it would be
a glorious stunt to master straight-shooting, broncho-
heaving, and steer-roping, and ride like a wind over
plains and up and down hill-slopes, and hustle after
rustlers and thieves, not because he cared about their
being wrong, or bad—who wasn't, to some extent?—
but because of the dashing joy involved in matching
his wits against them; and become a quick, muscle-
banded, unimpeded man. Of course, he'd get tired of
it after he could do it all perfectly, because it wasn't
something so big, and brainy, and shiny, that few
people could master it, but it would be pleasing just
for a while and just to show that nothing was too
arduous for *him*. He looked upon even his tap-dancing
as a compulsory prelude—a way of earning fairly large
sums and steeling himself against other eyes and ears
until he decided on a better form of expressing him-
self—the swollen, never-realizing, bragging-to-itself,
poorly equipped ambition that was to dominate the
tossing of his days.

Elizabeth thought that the cowboys were beautifully
brave but plain as mud when it came down to it—
interesting only when they were fighting, or riding, but
not men to be talked to, lived with. The rancher's
daughter captured most of Elizabeth's eyes—it *was*
thrilling to be fought over, and abducted, and coveted
by several men, regardless of how high a girl rated
these men, and the love-scenes with the cow-punching
hero, in arroyos and corrals, plinked the stringlets of

her heart and made her squeeze John's hand more tightly, since nothing is too impossible, or too thickly coated, to the screwed-up eyes of any youthful love.

Just after they had left the theater, John suddenly returned to the old theme.

"Gosh, I'll *bet* we're only a few blocks 'way from where you live. Why do I have to leave you on this same darn corner every night? Honest, I don't want to be fussy again, honest I don't, but gee, I wish you'd let me see you home now . . . it's *got* to happen some time."

He had none of his usual deeper resentment, but parting with her on a street corner meant physical restriction, whereas the vestibule, or porch, of her home could be a shelter for kisses and hugs—he hadn't had a chance to do more than hold her hand, or stroke her cheek, all evening, and it wasn't fair. This time she wavered within herself—she wanted to strain close to him too, and nine chances out of ten her parents and her sister would be in bed by now, and the neighbors might not notice them on the night- and tree-shadowed sidewalk . . . she just couldn't stand it any longer. Youth, no matter how oppressed and fearful it may be, can retain its caution only up to a certain point, when denial and accumulated seethings break into revolt!

"All right, I'll let you, Johnny"—her sigh had a world-pushing length and sibilance. "I don't think ma and pa are up now, and I *do* want to kiss you goodnight, and we can't do it here with all kinds of people watching us. But, Johnny, you must promise not to stay long on the porch, 'cause I don't want *any one* to find you there."

"Sure, I won't be long, honnikins, sure not"—his voice was delighted.

A-at la-ast this source of quarreling was gone—there wouldn't be a cloud in the heavens from now on! He tweaked her cheek and walked gayly down the side street, feeling like the cavalier in the fairy-tale, who had climbed to the supernaturally high tower where the inconceivably charming one was imprisoned —climbed after dozens of abortive attempts—for the contentious detail of not being able to escort Elizabeth to her home had become absurdly cankering and mag-nified to his youthful spirit. They passed a row of trees standing before dimly outlined wooden houses and walked into an area lit by a drug-store with a pool-room nestling beside it. A group of youths were standing in front of the drug-store window and good-naturedly scuffling over one boy's cap, which the others were hiding behind their coats—boys whom Elizabeth had high-hatted in their many underhand flings at "dating her up" ('what right did a nigger girl have to turn down *white* boys, who were doing her a bang-up favor by tagging after her? and she might be a shine, but doggone if she didn't look mighty like a white girl' —two pleasures rolled into one—'and some day they'd take the bean-pole out of her back, you just wait!') . . . Not cruel eighteen- and nineteen-year-olds—un-less cruelty is defined as that quality which also pos-sesses scolds, and Pucks, and hoax-players, and pinprickers—but ebullient with animal spirits and caring more to laugh at the "victim's" pique, or consternation, than really to harm him, and able to deal out raps without meaning them to be more than play-taps. Elizabeth and John halted near the drug-store entrance, debating on whether it was too late for her to have an ice-cream soda with him, which permitted chance—the great slayer, rewarder, and practical-joker —to stage an explosive exposure.

One of the lads had been introduced to John by Julius, at a Burnside Dance, and he whispered to his companions: "Say, I know that guy with her—name's Johnny Musselman. What d'yuh say, fellows? Let's ride him and see how he takes it."

"Aw, but he's li'ble to pitch into us."

"What the hell—we're six of us, ain't we? We won't hurt him none, see? Just wrestle him down if he pulls a scrap—it's a pipe."

The boy who knew John called out: " 'Lo, Johnny, what you doing way up here?"

"H'llo, I'm seeing my girl home."

Elizabeth tugged at John's arm and said desperately: "Let's be trotting, Johnny, oh, let's," but John remained standing and the other boy went on: "Bo-oy, you're picking 'em dark this season, ain't you?"

"What d'you mean, *dark?*"

"Goin' out with a nigger girl, that's what I mean."

"He-ey, are you saying my girl here's a nigger?"— a stunned scowl was on John's face.

"Ha-aw, ha-aw, tryin' to play innocent, are yuh? That's a ri-ich one, that is!"

The other boys cried out: "Guess they ain't so per-tic'lar down in Burnside," "Here, niggy, niggy, niggy," "She hooked a white kid a-at la-ast, that's hot stuff," "Gee, her old man'll be tickled to death now," "E-eeny, me-eny, mi-iny, mo-o, catch a ni-igge-er by the to-oe . . . if he ho-olle-ers, let him go-o-o."

A maniac rose in John's heart, since he disbelieved the boys and thought that they were taunting because Elizabeth was such a pronounced brunette, and his hands held a murderous crackling.

"You're a bunch of god-damn liars"—John stepped toward the boys, with Elizabeth hanging on to him and trying to hold him back.

Still laughing and throwing jibes, the boys prepared to pinion his arms as painlessly as possible—they were enjoying themselves and getting back at Elizabeth for her snubbings but they had no bile against him—when one of them spied a policeman a block away from the drug-store and walking toward it. His whispered: "Cheese it, cheese it, here comes a cop" was as effective as a wind on dry leaves—the boys scurried and dispersed down the shadowy lane of sidewalks and trees. John looked after them with a kinglike contempt, absolutely convinced now that they had been lying, but as he strode off with Elizabeth she drew her heart together, as a person might recoil from vomiting, and said: "It's true, Johnny."

Her voice was the woebegone sister of a whisper.

"What's true?"

"What they said . . . I'm a colored girl."

"You're wha-at?"

"A col . . . colored girl. One-eighth colored, any-ways."

They stopped on the walk and faced each other. Words are powerless to describe what broke out in his heart then—even the strongest of invectives, adjectives, and verbs would be too restrained to serve as symbols . . . ravings against her duplicity sheering into longings to comfort her and then whisked back to ravings a second later . . . hells of pain-surprise and butchered faith (hells to him at least, since one person's inner hyperboles may be but diversions and moderations to another) . . . a boyish cursing at life's barriers, grudges, back-stabbings . . . self-bewonderment —since she was a nigger, why hadn't she made his flesh creep a little in spite of the manlike enjoyment, like the nigger-women in the Red Light District, and why had it been just the opposite, sweeter than bon-bons when he touched her? . . . God, did anything hurt you unless you knew what it was? . . . anger at his loss of caste among the boys he knew—that bunch on the corner must still be splitting their sides, laughing at him and his calling them damn liars, and she had brought it all on him—the two-faced wench . . . dreading to face the hee-hees, snortings, and tongue-lashings of his family—that damn kid on the corner knew Julius and they were bound to find out . . . beaten-down desires to push everything aside and just

take her in his arms and swear to stick to her . . .
pities at her situation and boyish deductions of it. . . .
What a terrible fix she was in—too white to care to
take up with out-and-out coons and yet unable to marry
a white boy 'cause she had nigger-blood. . . . Oh,
hell, why couldn't she marry a white man?—the world
wouldn't cave in if she did . . . a feeling of panic that
didn't know where to turn . . . all of it bloated and
spurred on by the quickly maimed, unconsciously
theatricalizing, touchy, leaping-at-conclusions spirit
held by one kind of Youth. . . . Words can only catch
bald snatches of the cries that mobbed his heart, and
words cannot cope with the thrown-about stranger
within this mob—the unstained, scrutinizing, slimly
pervasive, seemingly helpless but dictating *Soul*, whose
final manifestation quells the wretchedness of emo-
tions, or leads them to determining violence, for rea-
sons unknown to human peerings! . . .

Pass by his spoken sentences of stuttering dismay
and dazed reproach, and her own resigned, scarcely
hearing, still and earth-quitting smotherings of emo-
tion—she had passed through *her* inferni during the
five weeks of her acquaintance with him and nothing
remained save the superfluous rattle of his blows and
. . . an enormous passive desire to stop living . . .
leave everything . . . take the possibility of peace that
nullifies all questions. On the following morning she
might wake up with some traces of armor again and
with the intent to plod on, but now her girlish self,

with its birth of harried maturity, cared only for extinction.

They are on the porch now—quick-breathing, bereft of words, and hollowed out by too much emotion spent in a short time. He had caught her throat and shook her—the mania against injustice within his spirit—as he had shaken life also, and said: "Why didn't you tell me 'bout it? Why'd you let me in for all this stuff? Why? Why?" but now he took her hand, with everything suddenly reduced to the flimsiest of whirlings and puff-ball plaints save the ever-new prisoner's-song of her body and the chugging of her heart. He kissed her, and in a twinkling, all of her doped, glumly suspended feelings disappeared, shot off into sky-rocketings of nerves within her. Hearts may imagine themselves demolished; unscalable walls may seem to block every path; and prejudices may howl, but the entire array can often be slain in the tenth of a second by the clasping of two fingers, or the pressure of lips on a cheek! The ever-hopeful, ever-intact survival of flesh —that medium which human beings shrink from and crave at the same time, using every verbalism and waistcoat to obscure the essential paradox!

John and Elizabeth forgot their respective selfishnesses—sadistic denunciation, and deceit turned to masochistic honesty—and strained breast and limb into the great, relatively selfless, excruciatingly synchronized rhythms of that physical love which must not be confused with the intransient dementias of lust—that love which no moralist, cynic, or intellectual moderator can ever quite understand.

.   .   .   .

Elizabeth and John had agreed to separate for two weeks, to see "if they could forget each other"—a perverted, longing-to-be-martyrized pleasure wrung from sadness, and a desire to show each other what fortitude they could exhibit and a little of a prompting to find out whether they could be sure of themselves, whether it wasn't all a bad dream and they'd wake up remembering nothing of each other—a nonsensical suggestion, this last, but sti-ill . . .

John's two weeks were too busy to give him much time for miserable feelings except at night before he went to bed, when he would often stare up at the ceiling as though it were an opaque mirror for future events —one which his eyes could somehow restore to a reflecting condition. He tried to school himself not to think of Elizabeth—the boylike expedient of turning his back on his own longings to see whether he wasn't self-sufficient after all . . . any simple effort to dismiss the pain of egotism unable to retire into itself, but she returned, like a ghost and a fleshly creature so intermingled with each other that reality itself became indecisive and he didn't know whether his love was a balky dream or a breathing, sorely-beset actuality. At such times he would take out a little snapshot of her and kiss it and moon over it and hold it still for minutes, much like a person pinching and bothering his emotions to see whether they were asleep, or instantly responsive. Oh, what a beautiful solution it would be to stop loving her—treat her as a nice, sympathy-deserving, already-captured girl, too well-enjoyed to be pursued any longer and living in a world far apart from his—a world that simply couldn't and shouldn't be reached. His heart would play with the idea for a while and then trail off into visionings of head-melting pettings with her; remembrances of her nose-tilted-for-just-a-second, near-to-grimacing smiles when she disapproved of something but thought it was funny; tremors left from his last jolting, tinglingly mixed-up, soul-hammering half-hour with her on the porch of her house; the sound-of-silk, enveloping drawl of her voice. . . .

He-ell, he loved her like sixty but he couldn't think of a single sound reason for it except that she came clean when she was provoked, and didn't have quite the silliness or serious dumbness of other girls, and had a mouth that was . . . was . . . hot ice-cream! . . . no other way of expressing it. The reasons were right enough to explain why he had gone with her but not why he couldn't break off now in the face of all the smashes waiting for him—if any guy ever knew just *why* he was in love he could change the whole world and cash in a million dollars on that secret!

Again, with the passing of days, her touch of negro-blood became less harrowing and formidable to him, in spite of the nigger-hate which had been planted in him by parents and youthful associates and against the instinctive retreating which was not nearly as strong in him as it is in utterly average men and women (average only in the sense of their being less complex!). . . . Say, why did God, or whatever was behind the earth, put negroes and whites on the small ball if He (or it) didn't want them to mix together? Again, what was there so horrible in black blood anyway, especially when it was just a drop or so? Again, if a girl looked white and acted white she shouldn't be forced to stay only with people who were mostly black and brown and behaved differently—she *belonged* more with white people then, and to keep her away from them was a dirty trick!

Slowly, he resolved to hang on to her with an invulnerable tenacity (like a bull-terrier, in his words)— even to marry her . . . pe-erha-aps—and show that *he* couldn't be slugged into joining the unfairness that greeted a nearly white girl of her beautiful kind, but he began to be much more concerned with the response of his family and the scorn, or kiddings, of boys and girls whom he knew, since his determination now changed these matters from possibilities to actualities. God, how they would all ride him on a rail and then jab at his hide for good measure—the one stand regarding which he could expect not a shred of sympathy, even from his mother. O-ow-w, it gave him the creeps. His folks would bawl the tar out of him and then drive him out of the house and never speak to him again if he refused to back down, and he'd have to give up all of his chums and acquaintances and then listen to their digs if he happened to run across them on the street, or any public place. A swell fix this was, and one that was liable to bust out at any time, since the kid who knew Julius would be only too eager to get ahold of his brother and tell him about the big joke on the Musselman family—people were never happy unless they could stir up something and then watch it safely from the sidelines.

John began to avoid staying at home, whenever he could, and to look at the other Musselmans with a strained expectation, and give one-syllabled replies to their joshings and beratings, and act like a hunted, self-effacing, haunted person, and while his parents thought that he was only sobering down to the work-aday world and losing some of his chattering kiddish-ness, his brother and sister—with the seventh-sense of youth, closer to one of their own age and more in-defatigably prying—were not so easily deceived. Though they 'didn't know just what was up,' they felt sure that it must be "terribly important" and that a girl was probably tied up in it and that it must be disgraceful in some way, since he was afraid to talk about it. They pestered him with questions and made inquiries among his Burnside pals, but his seemingly unmoved silences and slippings-off could not be pene-trated and the boys and girls of the neighborhood knew nothing except that 'they hadn't seen much of him for over a month.' Julius and Elsa could only watch and keep their peace.

The White Sox had gone on a road-trip and John was once more behind the bar at Sloan's saloon. The atmosphere was one of drippy, joking, cursing, utterly masculine planes and observances, with assorted degrees of fists pounded on the mahogany-varnished bar; tobacco-juice aimed at the tall, brass spittoons; cigars jutting from the corners of mouths (as though stage-hands were disrespectfully playing with magicians' wands); obscene postal-card pictures passed around with snickerings and eye-dilatings; rough tiffs over prices and local politicians and newspaper-sensations; assertions of general sexual mastery; discussions on the fine-points, detriments, and accessibility of local girls; jokes on the relations between different married pairs in the neighborhood, and how faithful the husband was, or what was missing in the wife; brawls, or their approaches, with invectives and fists ripping the air; hairy-chested lollings of the male, swilling and elevating himself to significance among his own kind; and tray-laden trips to the family-entrance backroom of the saloon, where men sat with the few indubitably fast women of the locality and engaged in alcoholic intimacies with them at the round, glistening tables.

All of this was a tonic to John—a super-masculine, overheated mud-leveled combination that buoyed him up and gave him an assumed, lip-stiffening maturity—he'd have to be a *man* all right if he was to down the troubles that were facing *him,* and Sloan's was certainly the place to put backbone and wisdom into a fellow. All of life seemed to undress in this saloon—to soak itself in verbal and arm-swinging confessions of sex leaping out of the moral cage; greed not

ashamed to rant and pant; "influence" operating to get
men out of jail, to secure sinecures for them, and even
to procure women for them; the generosity of loafers,
who treated to drinks until their last penny gave out,
in contrast to more respected local figures, who hated
to part with a dime; and upright, hard-working men
of the vicinity changed in a second—clowning, free-
talking, rambunctious. John could only sense the high-
lights in this scene, without being able to discover their
trends and implications with anything resembling an
unlaced use of words, and yet he pondered foggily over
them now and then and wrested bits of suspicion and
cynicism out of the pondering, and felt an uncompre-
hended, it's-too-much-of-a-fake, messy, overcrowded
problem in his heart—gee, there must be something
more beautiful and pure and honest about people than
what he saw and heard every day, but darned if he'd
met with much of it—Elizabeth . . . and two or three
other boys and girls who were pretty square and hefty
on the whole, and his family, of course—they might
be a little dumb sometimes, and they had their jeal-
ousies and stinginesses, but they were good-hearted and
well-meaning and straight at the bottom . . . or at
least he guessed they were. . . . No use to throw brick-
bats at your own family—you were part of them and
probably no better than they were, and to be affec-
tionate toward them was a warmly taken-for-granted,
soothing, huge necessity. He did love his ma—worked-
out-to-the-bone and sort of babylike in spite of her
fusses and orders; and his pa? . . . we-ell, a good

cuss when he was rubbed right, and always honest in his dealings with people . . . but . . . some tinder to strike up emotion just wasn't there. "Pa" was a largely unknown, uncompelling figure, barking first and then beaming when something tickled him—a four-hundred hand in an auction-pinochle game, or a prompt payment for a house-painting job, or a swell pfann-kuchen made by ma . . . but never squeezing into the heart, or making you miss him like the dickens—a man who had the guise of a faulty but fairly honored brother-to-a-Robot, to John. Even standing in the saloon, his father never quite relaxed, horseplayed, like the other men did, but stayed in the rear of the bar and whispered to Sloan. He'd give an ear to know what pa's whispering was about . . . funny gink, pa. . . .

He had arranged to meet Elizabeth on a Saturday night, in front of a Roseland church, and when the day arrived he felt bell-ringings in his heart, and a panacea for all human troubles—just do as you pleased and tell people to lump it, and then they'd finally wear themselves out and lay off you . . . grit winning against spite and opinionated buttings-in. . . . Oh, youth, youth, the life that kicks down your unweaponed, crudely combative hopes is the same existence that sponsors you—endless self-suicide and resurrection.

The explosion came at six o'clock when John returned from the saloon, with the I'm-King lyric in his heart. Julius, who had taken the day off because of an injured thumb, had run into his boy-friend, and the boy, filled with rumors and the desire to dramatize, had poured forth a swollen, mendacious tale—John was engaged to the nigger girl; her father had first tried to fight him but was now on good terms with him; John was known to have declared that niggers were as good as whites, if not better. Boiling over, Julius had hurried home and rallied the family around him, and they were in the midst of a war-conclave in the parlor when John walked in.

Tighten the climax now; avoid the storm of words in the vapidly fitted room with its horsehair furniture, gold-framed landscapes neither photographs nor impressions but dead . . . dead as the immortelles in the pink China basket on the mantelpiece—the storm of words that can be so easily guessed . . . bitter, profane, dictatorial ones from Julius and his father, who were ever twins in spirit and enunciation; John's mother, weeping, jaundiced, and yet trying to extricate him—her favorite boy had done wrong but he would, he must, come to his senses now; and blind flippancies from Elsa—if it had been a white girl, she'd have taken up for him to her last breath, 'cause *she* didn't think it was a crime for boys and girls to come together, but a co-ommo-on ni-igge-er, that was going too far!

And John—stammering, thrust-back, and word-ravished for the first ten minutes, his resolution made vaporous by the verbally swarming, hotly physical, armed pressure of his family—might have given in, for the time being at least, if Julius hadn't bellowed: "Any white guy 'at ses he'll marray a nigger wench, any

white guy like that is a son-of-a-bitch an' I don't care
if he's my own brother—I'll say it anyway."

The epithet assaulted John, like the tip of a white-
hot poker against the exact middle of his heart. . . .
Singular, maladjusted, human beings, who can remain
calm in the face of battlefield slaughterings, brutal un-
derpayments for work, the official murder of two, in-
nocent Italians—what not—but become enraged at
some empty phrase, or word, that carries with it a
twelve-year-old's effort at personal abuse (once I saw
a college Dean of Sociology turn to a berserk creature
when some one called him a god-damn bastard) . . .
John invited his brother to the backyard, where they
fought it out until the mother broke from her husband's
restraining arm and stopped the encounter. Then John
fled to his room, while the family, a little guilt-shaken
and reluctantly solicitous now in spite of the sense of
justified provocation, hovered around his locked door
and knew not what to do next.

He emerged with the peak of his cap down over his
eyes and a cold look on his face, paying no heed to
their softer words and striding out of the house. After
he met Elizabeth, they went out to a lonely, swamp-
enclosed, macadamized highway that stretched between
Roseland and the steel-mills on the shore of Lake
Michigan—a road disturbed only by occasionally rum-
bling trucks, and boys on bicycles. When their kisses,
wine-spillings of embraces, healing ejaculations and
avowals of fidelity had subsided to catch a second

breath—he told her of the family uproar and his fight
with Julius.

She had been squirming and railing at herself in the
peace of her own family during the past three weeks—
unable to tell her parents what had happened, or to
decide upon any liberating course of action—but now
she was lifted out of herself by the knowledge of his op-
pressive position. A longing for self-sacrifice—which
in most people is never more than egotism shaping a
sweet dream in its sleep and then waking up to ad-
vertise it—took hold of her heart and strove to doctor
its wounds. She battled with him for over an hour as
she strove to convince him that she would ruin his life
if they didn't separate, but his up-in-the-clouds, new-
hearted, pugnacious opposition slowly made her change
her mind—she was indeed more eager to change it than
her manufactured self-abnegation realized. Longings
for sacrifice are never full-fledged, or innate, in a girl
standing in her position, and when the boy whom she
loves piles fuel on her other desire for selfish pos-
session, the issue is ever decided in his favor.

They agreed to run away together on the following
Saturday—marry and find work in some distant city
—but the agreement came only after many qualms,
debates, and trepidations. They recognized the danger
of capture and arrest—hatred, officious men in uniform
clattering into the frail, unappreciated, lapis-lazuli
dream, with sightless, complaining families pressing
close behind them—but their inability to see any other
loophole in their present situation, and the sensual lyric

that raised chord on chord in their still unformed hearts, made an irresistible combination. Practical hopes rose also—if they married instantly they'd have a legal defense against the onslaught of policemen and parents, and if they lived quietly and worked hard it wouldn't be easy to find their hiding-place. . . . As they walked back to Roseland, she felt renewed and barely resolved—in spite of the touch of underlying fright that would not go—and like a person who had mastered the trick of standing erect on the point of a needle while he preserved a soldier-like, belt-tightening feeling—a feeling that was neither dutch-courage nor unimpeded bravery, but grazed the breath of each emotion and prayed for decision. . . .

During the following week, he lied to his family and curtly assured them that he had given up Elizabeth and cared to hear no more of the matter. Lying like a blue devil to his own flesh and blood—it hurt his marrow but it was either that or . . . give in to them. . . . "I *did* have a whopper of a crush on her. Sure, I'll admit that any time. I still like her lots too, you bet I do, and you'd all like her yourselves if you met her. She looks just like a white girl and you couldn't tell the difference in a million years if you saw her . . . not in a mi-illi-ion."

"Ye-e-eh, I know all that, I know it, but what you going to do 'bout keeping away from her?"—this from Julius.

"I'm going to stop seeing her, that's the honest truth, but it won't be 'cause I'm afraid of *you*. Just get that out of your head . . . I met her last Saturday and we made up our minds that it just wasn't right for negroes and white people to go with each other 'cause, well, 'cause they ought to stick to their own kind, no matter whether they like each other 'r they don't. That's all there is to it, but I've got this much to say. I don't want none of you to ride me 'bout it 'r mention her name from now on 'cause if you *do,* I'll pack up and clear out of here 'fore you can say Jack Horner!"

An attitude of instantly turn-tail submission would have made them suspicious, and one entirely resentful and independent would have kept the contention going full blast, and even a soft-tongued, family-loving recession would have tempered them but struck them as too good to be true. Nothing could have lulled them except his gruff, removed, pained and yet grudgingly resolved words. . . . 'Sure, he was still sore at them and still a little soft on this nigger girl and not quite himself yet, but he had forced himself to listen to common sense and realize that niggers and whites must stay in their places.'

After his first formal speech of renunciation, some dim, chafed, soul-dipped understanding of his possible suffering had gripped his mother and she had pulled his head to her shoulder and stroked his hair and murmured: "A-ach, you poor boy . . . mama knows what you feel . . . sure, mama knows, but your own folks got to come first, Johnny . . . your own folks is the nearest to you," while the rest of the family had looked away, reproached by the feeling that they had been too rough with him.

His mother's action had perturbed and weakened him for a while, since it disarmed him and made him feel that he was on the verge of knifing a family that really loved him in its interfering and eyeless way—made him feel like an inimitable scoundrel—but his love for Elizabeth fought against the invasion of softness. How about hurting her and himself and breaking up their lives—didn't that count? He wouldn't bring his family any lasting happiness by giving in to them now. They'd still go on to the troubles and bothers waiting for them in their own lives, and they'd still quarrel about other things among themselves and with him—all that they'd have would be the passing satisfaction of having kept him a slave to their ideas and their loving selfishness. He strengthened again and even wrested a gloomy zest from his part of an "expert actor"—if you *had* to be underhanded you might as well make a good job of it, and besides, the whole damn world was always ready to crush you whenever you dared to show your real face, and the task of outwitting this concerted opposition gave you an on-your-toes militancy (not his own words but their counterparts).

He had arranged that they would both sneak their baggage out of their homes around midnight, when the families were asleep, and then meet at the railroad depot downtown, and when Friday evening came—the night before their intended departure—he began to assort his belongings and eye his suitcase, with an impatient, adventurous, and more-frightened-than-he-cared-to-admit tug of the heart. He was up early on the next morning, waiting to catch the mailman outside of the house, in case she had sent him some last message of instruction, and when he received a thick letter addressed in her handwriting he rushed back to his room and almost tore the paper in two, in his haste to open the envelope. The letter read as follows:

"VERY DEAREST JOHNNY:

"I don't know how to begin and I don't know what to say and I've cried and cried till I can't cry no more. I know how you'll feel when you get this terrible letter and my hand is shaking so I almost can't write it, but when you do get this letter I'll be on the train with my folks. I told them all about us, I just told them everything and didn't leave out a single thing because I couldn't hurt them like I thought I could. They was awfully sweet and nice to me, really they was, and they showed me how you and me could never, never have any happiness if we ever married, and I asked them why they had married then and they said it was because ma had been a poor orphan when she was very young and she had been working for some white people down in New Orleans, and those white people, they was beating her and making her work so she couldn't stand up no more, so pa, he rescued her and he gave her a home and maybe saved her from something terrible, because you see she was very desperate then. And they said maybe they would never have married if they had

known what they was in for, and they said they didn't
want me to go through all the bad, mean things that
had come to them, and so you see, you see, I couldn't
go through with you and me running away then, be-
cause I could tell so plain how we didn't have a single
chance to be happy. So good-by, my very dearest
Johnny, and you never forget me because I'll never,
never forget you. Please don't be mad at me and please,
please don't try to follow me and don't try to find out
where I've gone, because we haven't told anybody and
we are going because there would be lots of trouble
with your family and because you and me would not be
able to stay away from seeing each other if we was
living so close together. So good-by again, my very
dearest Johnny, and I am sending you a thousand
kisses, though I know they won't cheer you up, but
I am sending them anyway, and I'll kneel down and
pray every night for you to be happy and find some
sweet girl and be good to her. And just remember that
I'll always love you, always and always, and forever.

"ELIZABETH.

"P.S. Please, I want you to go on with your dancing
and be a great, famous man some day, and remember,
you are the only man I'll ever love.

"E."

He read the blotted, closely scrawled letter ten times,
and if you can imagine howlings, snivelings, whimper-
ings, rankling silences, flogged into a pulsating huddle,
in which their separate identities became almost extinct,

you will discern the condition of his heart. Then wild
snatchings at possible deception came . . . one of his
family might have imitated her handwriting; her
parents might have forced her to write the letter and
she might still be living in Roseland; she might have
sent it to test his determination and see if he wouldn't
back out. He dashed out of the house and boarded
a street-car for Roseland—his family thought that he
was only hustling down to Sloan's because he had over-
slept—with his mind made up to beard her parents in
the house, if they were still there. After he had pounded
on the house-door, and peered into the ominously dark
front room, through windows shade-covered almost to
the bottom, a girl from the family living on the second
floor of the house came down. 'Yes, the Harrisons had
moved away yesterday.' 'No, she didn't know where
they'd gone, though she'd heard something about it
being New York City.' 'You see, the neighbors had
found out that Elizabeth Harrison was going to marry
a white boy, and some of the men-folks had visited her
father and told him they'd make it mighty hot for him
if he didn't clear out'—she looked carefully at John
and wondered whether he might not be the boy in
question. John, shrinking from possible derision, as-
serted that he was from a coal-company and had come
for an order, after which he walked away, with the
muscles in his chest shaking till they seemed as un-
availing as tissue-paper . . . filling the bright morn-
ing with a dark impotence . . . incensedly unwilling
to live and yet too self-limp to die.

He made his way to the tree where he had first spied her and threw himself headlong upon the grass and felt that all things had ended save the motions and sounds of other people impervious to his living death. The death of a boy did happen there on the grass, and a prematurely sour, planning-to-retaliate man, who would never quite recover from this first blow, did shuffle down the railroad tracks in the midst of a sun-bathed afternoon.

．　　．　　．　　．　　．　　．　　．

John still looked at the window in the rear wall of his cell—looked with the fixity of an idol-worshiper whose unkind god was a barred panel of sky and cloud. Blue and black and gray—let us have venom for breakfast. The preacher will call it justified indignation, and millions of deluded dwarfs, reading of the ceremony, will feel pity, or angrily exonerated approval, according to how well or how poorly the animal in their natures has been stifled. But blue, black, and gray— one elated color, one lack of all colors, and one merging of whiteness and death to blanketed reflection— are more potent than yellow, red, and green, because they are less human, less earthly, and more in sympathy with the light and shade of minds that care to revolve, and with the wide curve of cryptic matters that stand and move beyond the self-acclaimed circlings of a little globe in space. . . .

Ten seconds had flown by—seconds of remembrance so quick and searing that hours shrank to fractions within them—*for time is only the inevitable dream with*

*which motion of every kind assumes the attributes of
advancing and perishing, and if all things were to stand
forever still, time would disappear. . . .*

A robin lit on the outer ledge of the window, looked
in for a second, with head cocked sideways, and then
flew off, as if one glance at the sinister, prose-angled cell
had served to shoot the bird into the air, though it had
only decided to resume its insect-grubbing. The bird
whisked back to John the memory of another robin
which had figured in the culmination of a past
episode. . . .

He was working as a cotton-picker on a plantation
ten miles out of Libertyville, Texas—aged twenty-five
now and changed, for the time being, to an addled,
catch-as-can, ribald drifter, though ghost-walkings of
the boy he had been shouldered themselves in at crucial
times.

A synopsis of the intervening years would show a
steady retrogression of the body and the emotions dis-
puted by an almost equally steady increase in mental
speed and protective proclivities. However, this bet-
terment of thought had made him only more pos-
sessed with the knavish, befuddled, self-primping,
idolatrous futility of life, which was prone to turn its
fairest cheek and costliest raiment to the gaze but could
strip itself to claws and broken laws in a second's in-
terim. . . .

Returning to John, his feeling of life-futility was
abetted by the fact that he was neither a creator nor
a treadmill performer but a man of troubled impulses

and partly keen perceptions, who lacked a freeing talent and was consequently the prey of more solidified and decisive elements in the life outside of him. He had passed through a year of tap-dancing on the smaller vaudeville circuits, consorting with coarsely mechanized women and palling about with smutty-tongued, near-sighted, fair-weatherish male friends, but quart on quart of whisky—which brings a who-the-hell-cares spirit—and the inability to rise in his profession, made him desert the stage. Of course, the whisky would have been powerless if it had not drenched a receptive substance, which was the grudge left in his heart by the loss of Elizabeth, but his failure to advance in tap-dancing was also caused by the lack of an inherent adaptability—the inspired fusion of muscles, bones, and initiative, which divides the top-notcher from the minor performer. John had learned the routine steps of the profession but could not stamp beyond them, try as he would. Some extra-springiness, some hurrying balance in which intention rules over matter, simply wasn't there—a lack which dominates obscure vaude-villians and sometimes turns them into scandal-monger-ing newspaper columnists. In John's case, however, it shunted him to more openly lazy expedients—gambling with cards and dice; working a week or two as a barker, or a dance-hall host, to procure the money for these games; and sponging on the members of his former craft—a hesitant approach to a racketeer. Self-disgust and penitent boredom rose within him nevertheless, ricocheting back and forth with the luck, or disfavor, brought by each day, but making themselves more and more felt on the whole.

Then, after a terrific fight in a cabaret, caused by an infatuated, stupid, sex-ridden girl who had failed to tell him that she was married and that a jealous husband was hunting for her, he grew tight-jawed and self-abusive as he nursed his bruises in his hotel room. Christ, he was frittering his life away and evolving into an uncaring, hop-skip-and-jump numbskull of a cake-eater and a lunchroom-cowboy, and what for?—a rattle-tongued, unreliable jane now and then, and natty clothes for which he had to spend his last penny—since the lack of a front was equal to self-murder, in the lower Broadway mob in which he mingled—and boozing every night to keep himself from realizing how worthless he had become.

A-aw, that was all very well, but why think about something that had no chance of being escaped—something as fickle and yet unmistakable as the spots on a dice-cube. He wouldn't work as a manual-laborer for small wages; hotel-clerking and cashier-plugging meant long hours and confinement; he had no talent for high things like writing, or drawing. . . . Slide by, John—graft, lie, work the dames, act big over highballs . . . and detest yourself, but not strongly enough to break away from habits and finales! Well, he'd quit Broadway just the same, leave it fla-at—it was lessening his health, pitching him into trouble, and making a third-rate moocher out of him.

He had drawn away from his family and scarcely

ever wrote to them, and he knew that they regarded
him as a mystifying ne'er-do-well, and it would take
too big a gulping of pride to return home now. . . .
He took to the freight-cars and passenger-blinds, bum-
ming his way from town to town in the middle-west
and south—begging, thieving a little (conscience-
bothered but doing it doggedly because indolence had
become an imperative morphine), and working two or
three weeks at menial jobs when hunger intervened.
Then he had received six months in jail for vagrancy—
an unusually severe sentence because, with a sizzling-up
of his former adolescent spirit, he had talked back to
the judge—and the vermin, dirt, and calloused squalor
of his imprisonment had snapped what was left of his
backbone, for the time being—a spine that was to be
absent for a long period. His battered, smirched dreams
of being different, of attracting attention and plaudits,
reduced to vestiges, became completely wiped out, and
a sneering, enduring, sensuality-pursuing spirit took
their place. . . .

Critics sometimes disparage an author with the claim
that his people show no character-development, though
frequently men and women of forty are fundamentally
just what they were at eighteen, with the exception of
purely exterior traits and quirks donated to mind and
heart by realistic experience. The promulgation that
such people do not exist, or are too uninteresting to
write about, is nonsensical—the surface variations at-
tached to a definite, one-colored trend can be just as
diverting as those which lead down to more basic up-

heavals and reversals. John was never to lose the tend-
encies flashed in his earliest youth—saint, dreamer, and
maniac in a stuttering free-for-all—and his downfalls
and reassemblings were to be no more than undeter-
mining phases and phrases in this process. Now, just
over twenty-five, he was still the boy of eighteen, whose
mind had labored fruitlessly and whose heart had ob-
jected to life underneath a tree, except that the finer
edge of hope had gone, and recalcitrances had grown
sneaking and apathetic by turns, and sentimentalities
were temporarily mortgaged to unheeding realities.

He had come to the plantation from Houston, Texas,
where he had worked a week for a house-wrecking con-
cern which was demolishing an old hotel—carrying
out boards and plaster débris. Nails in the boards
continually jabbing his hands caused him to give up the
job—catch *him* getting bloody scratches for fifteen a
week. Then with a tongue-in-the-cheek, pestered spirit,
he had joined the Salvation Army in Houston and
pounded the drum, and railed at sinners during street-
meetings, but his conscience started to gnaw at him.
Taking up for God, when he didn't mean it and there
might indeed be a God: he wasn't sure one way or the
other—this was a low-down stunt, not to speak of the
punishment that might come in some Here-After (Hell
smacked more real than Heaven—more like the earthly
idea continued and swelled up, except that *everybody*
got it on earth!).

He had hopped a freight and had been thrown off
at Libertyville at five in the morning—an August morn-

ing that was dewily cool now but would soon be sun-
stifling and dust-sifted. He tried to catch an hour's
sleep on a clump of wild-sorrel and milk-weeds along-
side the tracks, but ants and ticks were too numerous
and he had to rise and limp down the rails. Most Texas
villages were hostile and death-on-panhandlers, but he
was too tired and hungry to care about what would
happen to him.

The town had two, wooden, gray-painted saloons, not
open yet; a few streets that were merely clay-dirt roads,
with trampled ground-paths for sidewalks; one- and
two-story wooden houses holding a tumble-down
peeling-off, morosely pointed effect; and a collection
of hovels, shanties, tents, and huts as weak-looking
as match-boxes—the negro-quarter. The village would
have given one the impression of life crawling, moiling,
just enough to escape from the full penalty of laziness
—real work was largely restricted to the outside planta-
tions—and bartering unspiritedly, with little of a play-
ing desire except among the youngest children, and even
they often stared into the air as though trying to re-
member that they were alive. John had the feeling of
a mere mold of seeking-flesh as he slunk up one of the
disorderly village-streets shaded by cottonwood trees,
bordered by lean-down picket-fences, and dotted with
occasional tin cans and bottles in the gullies that lined
its paths.

He skirted around the jail—the only brick structure
in the village and a foreboding, flat-topped coop—and
came to a small lunch-wagon lit by coal-oil lamps. He

went in and asked for a dish-washing job and the
proprietor—a sallow-brown, black-mustached, long-
nosed man in a dirty white apron and blue-gray work-
shirt—looked him over as though an insect might need
to be stepped on. Fortunately for John, the region was
short of cotton-pickers, with a big crop fully grown,
because the negroes had been leaving in large numbers,
lured by the higher wages in an adjacent locality. The
sheriff and the tradespeople of the village were trying
to draft hoboes by offering them a choice between
cotton-picking and jail, and the lunch-wagon man "put
it up" to John and said: "Wa-all, stranghuh, weah shy
on pickahs this season, raght shy, and we've got a
smaht ol' jail heah, lousy's Mandy's wrappah. Maybe
you'd rawthah do a stretch uh *wuhking* 'stead uh doing
sixty in the coop—reckon so-o?"

John hastily agreed with the man, and then another
man walked in—a lanky, dodging-faced, weather-burnt
man, with screwed-up eyes that never looked straight
at anybody and a weakly thick mouth and a shock of
uncombed, mouse-brown hair. The man wore gray
cotton pants tucked into high-laced shoes and a high-
peaked, broad-brimmed, black hat and a black shirt
open at the throat—farmerish and yet with a city-aroma
hanging to him. He engaged John as a picker and
they went to one of the saloons, where he swilled
whisky as though it were water and treated John with
a heavily patronizing sportiveness—"pooah devil, ah'll
get you drunk and see how you cut up." John hated
the man's tone, especially when the other said: "Co-ome

a-awn, put some gi-ingah intah you—ah ain buying
drinks fo' no souah-face!" and he proceeded to spill
his drinks on the floor, to keep his head, because his
soul sniffed the fact that he might try to murder this
man otherwise—the maggoty son-of-a-bitch, thought
he'd hired a baboon to laugh at, did he?

The saloon was divided into sections for negroes
and whites—a boundary as sacred as God to the negroes
but crossed by the whites whenever they pleased, not
to drink with the negroes but to summon them for
work, or command them to make less noise. Lit by
incandescent gas-lights in oval globes furnished by
small tanks; bearing a wooden floor where dirt had
become ingrained; and decorated by shotguns, squir-
rel-pelts, bottles, lithographs of women with only the
top-bust or stockinged legs exposed—the community's
moral front was thicker than that of American cities
—the saloon had a callowness that zigzagged between
lewdness and the less sexual disporting of simple coun-
try men drinking to dispel the heat and the sweaty
trampings, tramplings, and snorings within their lives.

Joe Vile, John's employer, passed into a plaint-bab-
bling, self-caressing drunkenness, and John's mur-
derous up-flamings shrank to a mood distantly related
to pity but separated from pity by a lifeless inattention.
Now that Vile was gurgling and flattened, what did the
man matter to him? . . . Vile was a coward of the
first rank but intensely unaware of it. He could squash
a beetle and think that he had stepped on a scorpion.
He was too crawling to be dishonest and too lame-

souled for honesty—he could have stolen ten cents, with glee, and then returned a thousand dollars because he dreaded detection and capture. He had a woman tucked away beneath his man's hide, yet he was seventy per cent masculine. He could be kind to a dog and incredibly brutal to his wife. He was too perturbed to dare to be lascivious and too sex-denied, and willing, to be moral. He sought none of the negresses in his neighborhood—in common with *most* of the white men near him—because the majority of them were utterly repulsive, and he feared the probable roars of laughter that might attack him if he were caught—"What's gummed up—youah woman getting sick uh you?"

He deluged John with complaints. 'Abe Spector, the main-cheese, who owned the plantation and from whom Vile rented fifty acres, was a hard's-nails, dyed-in-cotton rascal; the climate was killing him—he could kick himself for having quit his job as a warehouse-watchman in Houston three years ago; cotton-raising was the Devil's picnic; Spector charged outrageous for mules and produce so's to always keep a man in debt to him; niggers were good pickers but a man needed a rawhide to get the bastards to work any; 'twasn't natural for a man to live 'thout seeing no pretty gals—not bo-othe-er 'em, yuh know, but just look 'em over some.' John grunted assents, or shoved him away. . . . Finally, Vile sat in a poker-game for hours while John looked on with a mood that had a blurred affinity to melancholy, but was too decomposed for any vital emotion. Yawping, squinting, and straining over dimes and quarters—he'd done the same things hundreds of times, and why?—to kill time with the only thing left when a guy's heart and mind had nothing else to chew over. In the big poker-games it was fighting to coax enough money to live on, or make a splurge with your girls, but in the dime and quarter ones you used fifty-two pasteboards to color your emptiness. Money on the hidden sides of cards—braah, the only mystery left when everything else was far too obvious.

When twilight came, Vile lumbered out of the saloon with John, proud as a Viceroy over his ten-dollar winnings given by the invisible Sovereign; boasting of the full-houses and flushes he had held; digressing on the bluffs he had put over on ace-high, or a pair of jacks—the weakling, who loves to pose as the great, nervy darling of chance. Vile's buggy was hitched to a wooden water-trough—spattered with mud which had turned to a hard yellowish-gray, and bearing a rolled-up, black top, like those on perambulators, and large wheels that wobbled on their axles. The broken-down russet mare in front of it was whinnying and stamping hoofs, for Vile had not fed her since morning. With his almost slobbering kindness to animals—a subconscious form of repentance for his lack of softened egotism to humans whom he could safely abuse— Vile fastened a bag of oats to her nose and patted her sides and rubbed liniment on a sprain on one of her forefeet. One may often notice this tendency in public-spots, where women with heavily calcimined, pettily unimaginative, sexually bridling faces, spend an hour, or two, unbrokenly feeding peanuts to pigeons and squirrels, and cooing over the cuteness of the animals, and scarcely ever glancing up, as though the remainder of the world had disappeared.

Vile and John drove out into the country just as dusk was settling over Nature's crimes and gala-bedeckings, and the narrow dirt road twisted on hills, dales, and little wooden bridges over ravines. Clearings, from fifty to one hundred acres, stood bordered by forests of pines, birches, oaks, pecans, and hickory trees, with occasional willows and magnolias. The clearings were mostly covered with cotton-bushes, whose white flecks showed with a dim creaminess hedged by green under the moonlight, but sometimes corn and alfalfa fields rustled drowsily to the motion of breezes. The night-cry of insects dominated the air—that never-broken, eerily trembling piping and humming which does not slay the country silence but gives it the quality of vastly separate listening. In a city, night-sounds suck up all that there is of silence, but in the country they seem powerless to assimilate an inaudible background. The underbrush and trees were alive with cracklings and swishings, for the region still held a fair measure of raccoons, 'possums, polecats, foxes, and squirrels, while a few snakes and wildcats still lurked in the deeper ravines and swampily impenetrable glens between the hills. One-story wooden farmhouses, little more than overgrown sheds with black-shingled roofs rising in a low angle, stood be-

side, or near, the road, at quarter- or half-mile in-
tervals.

Vile dozed off every now and then and John had to
shake him and shout—John had not the vaguest idea
of how to reach Vile's farm and he foresaw hours of
being lost in this dark, strange region, but Vile finally
mumbled: "S'all right, Fanny knows the way hum 'n'
you jus' giver slack rein 'n' whipah when she gits too
slow." He slumped into a groaning sleep and John
eyed him with a speculative aversion. How easy it
would be to take his money, dump him along the
road, drive back to Libertyville, and hop a freight, or
passenger. The impulse became still-born. In spite of
his manias, bindings, and muddles, John was neither a
renegade nor a preying skulker but more a harried
wastrel full of thoughts and dreams that led to no con-
crete expression, and his sizable conscience would not
let him steal openly unless his belly was collapsing.
During his life on Broadway he had often engaged in
small swindlings such as playing with loaded dice, or
steering a simp into a cabaret and pocketing a per-
centage of the raised prices, but in a locality where
almost every one practiced some form of devious graft,
or "getting by," he had told himself that he could not
survive unless he acted like the people around him.
Even then his conscience had jerked and murmured
when he was not sneering-full of alcohol, and this
motivation had given its push to his final departure.
. . . "No, let this fool keep his dirty wallet—I won't
be a sneak unless I have to, to keep from starving!"

The horse stopped in front of a low, small house, with a tall cedar growing in front of it, and payed no attention to John's whip-strokes. John woke up Vile, after much tugging and yelling, and found that they had reached the latter's farm. They drove into the dull-red, leaning-over barn and a mongrel dog rushed out with threatening barks but quieted when it smelled its master. Vile shook its paws, patted it and crooned over it, and as John watched, he relented a little—maybe this man wasn't low-down but just a weak-sister who loved to brag his head off.

At this point, the mingling of narrative, essay, and poem will become suggestive and disorganized for the time being, to avoid the host of descriptive and analytical details which so many people relish but which are distasteful to the present writer. . . .

Canvas-bound straw pallet in a corner of the kitchen. . . . "Las' pickah done got it kina lousy, but we'll soak it in coal-oil aftah sun-up." . . . Lice, the dinosaur, the saber-tooth tiger, barnacles, the octopus, bed-bugs, sewer-rats, alligators—Nature, with her jumble of impersonally cruel accidents culminating in the most efficiently cruel one of all—Man—and given a false order and purpose by evolutionists: Nature, that self-unaware, behemothlike earthliness, became surprised at having devised creatures with *souls,* creatures that could slowly learn to protect themselves against most of her ravages. The surprise may lead to some spectacular dénouement some day. . . . Waking up at five-thirty in the dreary kitchen with its black iron, wood-burning

stove and zinc pails and tubs and tar-papered walls.
. . . Corn-meal, black molasses, fried bacon, and cof-
fee. . . . Ruth, Joe's wife—a dumpy, short woman of
thirty-two, with a fear-wheedled, scarcely-daring-to-
smile, unhoping ghost of youth on her brownly plump
face. . . . Brown hair tied to a knot on the top of her
head; wide mouth with little lust in it; brown eyes
that were seven-eighths blind and just efficient enough
in the other eighth to take in the homely images stand-
ing around her. . . . Her eleven-year-old son, George—
face like his father's; little scared voice, and with child-
like dreams already gasping; staggering through a day
of man-sized jobs—chopping wood, grooming the pairs
of horses and mules, caring for three pigs, pitching hay.
. . . Starting to pick at six in the morning with the
dew still heavy on the cotton-bushes and the crows saw-
ing their discords and a freshly pungent, overwarm
smell in the air. . . . Dragging the canvas bag that was
strapped around his right shoulder and trailed on the
ground, John plucked at the seed-weighted, white fluff,
but the points of the half-open cotton pods scraped
and dug into his hands, and the cotton clung to these
pods and needed two or three tugs to extract it. The
negroes, picking like humanly disguised machines, were
already at the end of their rows while he was hardly
one-third of the way down his. At the end of the day
he had picked only ninety-five pounds, whereas even
the slowest negro could gather three hundred without
undue sweating. Vile grumbled and spoke of "firing

him" if he couldn't do better, and John became desperate. . . .

The cotton was weighed on a scale hooked to the branch of a tree at one corner of the field, after which it was dumped on the ground and carted away late in the afternoon. On the next day, when the noon hour came, John noticed that this large heap was left unguarded and unwatched as the pickers, Vile, and Jed Marshall, one of Spector's overseers, ate their lunches beneath a distant clump of trees. John knelt behind the less exposed side of the heap and crammed his bag with cotton, after which he crawled into the cotton-bush rows until he had reached the middle of the field, where he stood erect and went through the motions of imaginary picking. The trick had a simple audacity which, aided by luck, managed to escape detection day after day—if any of the distant lunch-eaters had happened to turn their eyes toward the weighing-tree at the exact moment when John was filling his bag, or if any man from the Spectors' "main shack," or cotton-gin, had caught John by surprise, he would have been knocked down and ordered out of the region, for sternness toward small and crude dishonesties was the white man's reliance here, "to keep the niggahs' fingahs in theyah place." However, luck—which is a secretly orderly system so veiled by senseless semblances of deviation that humans cannot comprehend it—was working in John's favor, and he continued his bag-stuffings for two weeks and then stopped when he had become sufficiently proficient in his picking to turn in

over two hundred and fifty legitimate pounds every
day. . . .

As he wrenched his muscles into the third week, his
revolted and spurred-on mood became more inured
and self-heedless—the sun scalding his hide; bag-strap
biting into shoulders and back as he dragged one hun-
dred pounds along the ground; wood-ticks, mosquitoes,
ants, making him dig nails into flesh; endless corn-
meal and bacon; no diversion at night except sleep—
it was a good, hard wrestle with life, and left him too
fagged-out to do any thinking, which was a negative
virtue, since thinking only gave him a hedged-in, un-
promising, aggrieved unrest. And all of it wasn't flesh-
grating. He liked to hear the negroes sing as their
hands darted over the cotton-bushes. . . . "Go-ot tuh
see mah Sayrah, ev'ry ni-ight. Said ah'm gointa
see mah Sa-ayra-ah, hug her tight. Said ah'm go-ot
to see mah Sa-ayra-ah, ev'ry ni-ight. Said ah'm gointa
see mah Sa-ayra-ah, hu-ug he-er ti-ight. . . . It takes a
lit-tul ma-an, tuh do the midnight gri-i-ind. It takes
a lit-tul, lo-ong-le-egged, sa-assa-afra-as ma-an tuh do
the midnight gri-i-ind. . . . Pick dat co-otto-on, pick
it fa-ast. A-all youah mi-isry's go-one an' pa-ast. Ain'
no troubles gointa la-ast, ef you pi-ick dat co-otto-on,
pi-ick i-it fa-a-ast. . . . Ole man cotton, he's a son of
a bitch. Makes the cu-ullu'ud ma-an wu-uhk 'n' makes
the whi-ite ma-an rich. But ole man cotton don' know
which is which, an' he spre-eads raght o-ou-ut jus' lak
a son of a bitch. . . . We-ent tuh Ho-ou-usto-on tuh
ta-aya-ah o-off a tri-ick. Didn't ta-aya-ah it o-off bu-ut

ah go-ot da-amn si-ick. We-ell ah'm sa-ati-isfi-ied, ca-au-use ah go-otta a be-ee. . . . Blo-ow o-on youah ha-awn, Ga-abreeul, blo-ow i-it lo-ou-ud. We'll a-all be adancin' a-an' aste-eppi-in' pro-ou-ud. No-obo-ody-y's gointa st-ay fum o-out da-at cro-ow-wd. O-O-Oh blo-ow o-on youah ha-awn, Gabreeul, bl-o-ow i-it lo-ou-ud."

Funny negroes—they seemed to be happy but they weren't, and less often they seemed to be down-in-the-mouth but the next minute they might be ya-ahya-ahing like a locomotive-bell. They had a passion for making the best of things and extracting some cheer from their scorching work, but that was how they kept themselves from nursing grudges, or sinking into a lie-down-'n'-die feeling—from becoming too aware of their serflike condition. But it didn't always work—after they had lapped up enough white mule, or when some unusually raw stunt was put over on them by the whites—such as cheating them out of most of their pay, or cornering one of their women and lining up on her—they grew nastily silent and disobedient and then (so he'd heard) they raped a white girl, or murdered a white man, and hell broke loose for a week or two till they were beaten down again. The older whites never went near the negresses, but sometimes their sons, lads from eighteen to the early twenties, sallied out in a gang at night "to pick off a coon" walking alone on one of the roads. The number of accessible white girls in the region were few, and the blood of the younger blades could not always stay cool, and such marauderings were the safest way of dismissing the enforced abstinence.

John couldn't hate the negroes, or like them strongly —they were uncommunicative, strangely interesting, but untrusted aliens to him, and while a moderate ratio of sympathy was compulsory as he shared their bondage in the fields, he felt that his white blood would make them misunderstand any friendly overtures on his part —they lumped all white men together, and how could they be sure that he wasn't just as bad as the other whites in the place? Funny, too, how the whites here treated the negroes—joshing with them, slapping them on the back, and even doing them offhand favors sometimes, but underneath, watchful, frostily congealed, and even picayunish in their exactions (the last adjectives are the author's, since he feels justified in interpolating himself those thoughts and feelings which his characters could not adequately shape). . . .

John often thought of Elizabeth in connection with the negroes around him, and then an unfathomable emotion would possess him—too hopeless to be bitter, too checkmated to be resigned, too overwhelmed by the past to rule more than an active third of his heart, but singeing and sputtering nevertheless. God, if she was like these dark, coarse, enthralled children then his eyes were out, but still she was called a nigger and treated like an unclean pariah. . . . "Aren't you through with wailing about that, John? You see how much good it's ever done you. Mixed seven-eighths milk with a few drops of coffee and still called it coffee, the miserable

bastards." . . . What was she doing now?—married
but still weeping over him sometimes when she was
alone; or shunning other men and carrying a heart
like a stone (yes, it didn't *always* happen in books, in
spite of the damn few people who did it); or going out
with negroes and laughing, dancing, until the memory
of him suddenly gashed her to stillness; or really loving
another man, without a thought of John Musselman?
. . . In spite of the small-time sophistication which five
intervening years had given him—that of the beset,
disabused, and often mulcted underdog—and his dal-
liances with tens of women, he was still a rabid senti-
mentalist in the pits of his being and Elizabeth would
always remain to him the stainless goddess, who had
been abducted from him by the soiled, clawing preju-
dices of a world. Cynical pinchings might take him—
"Cripes, another guy mugged her a few weeks after she
left, for all I know," or "G'wan, she had her good time
with me *then*, but I'll wager she wouldn't even recog-
nize me now"—but they never lasted for more than
the time it took to say them to himself and they were
always instantly superseded by a heartsick but rallying
worship of her—a determination to make her the one
person whom he would always enshrine against a be-
traying earth. . . .

The end of the third week was enlivened by the
appearance of two white girls picking in the second
field to which John had been assigned, since he was now
working for Spector though still living at the Vile farm-
house. They were chits of fifteen and sixteen—Anna-

belle and Florence Owens, nicknamed Belle and Floh
—and their mother, who had lived on a neighboring
rent-farm before the death of her husband, now worked
as a cook in the Spector home where the three lived in
one dark hole behind the kitchen. They were both
brunettes and their skins had been darkened by the
sun until only a breath of nut-brown clearness saved
them from an Ethiopian duskiness. Belle was curved
scarcely more than a lad and her little face was gnomish
and stub-nosed beneath the dark-brown hair that
dropped in pig-tails over her back, but Floh, while
almost bosomless, was fully curved below the waist
and had the face of a farmyard bacchante and a virgin
trying so hard to be unaware of each other's presence.
Her little face with its half straight nose, and loosely
beseeching lips that drew near to vacancy sometimes,
was ineffably ignorant, and yet a little meanly wise in
sexual ways—bad words overheard from the men;
warm sensations left by Fred Spector, son of the plan-
tation-owner, who was always wrestling with her under
the pretext of making her take back some name she
had called him; scufflings among negro men and women,
which she had beheld with a curiosity that was strained
at the bottom and properly denied on the top. To such
a girl, sex was inevitably an unnaturally proportioned,
wickedly glowing, secretly longed-for rescue. Barely
able to read and write, and with her life wedged between
slaveries and semi-monthly trips to Libertyville, where
the only excitements were a cheap brooch or a bottle

of soda-pop, what else was left but deliciously goaded though lip-banished se*x*? . . .

You preaching, cautious morons, who attempt to rule the lives of young people—you take shaky-hearted girls and steep them in physical toil; deny them access to any of the daintier and finer shadings of thought and emotion; strip their lives of all intangibility save the hollow admonishings of the bible; see that they are introduced to sex via the sentences scribbled on out-houses, or the smutty solicitations of equally pent-up boys, and then you become "aghast" when they are discovered to be wallowing in flesh behind the scenes; or you make a belated effort to reform them; or you run to the hypocritical "solution" of companionate-marriage; or you yawn and profess a faintly smiling disinterest (in the manner so popularized by "The New Yorker" of our day); or you try to save your faces with rantings, or "sensible" entreaties (a belated arrival of "sense," indeed!). . . .

John often spoke to Floh but he had little desire to court her—up-to-date sex had brought him only wild parties turned to prosy disillusionments when the next morning, the next week came; tussles with jealous men; the Great Pain in Burnside—a cut-and-dried furor. This was his present mood and he welcomed his toiling vacation from sex, so his conversations with Floh were comradely and innocently jesting on his part, though she tried to draw him on in her brusque, raw manner because she liked the shape of his face and the amazing fact that he kept his hands and most of

his looks to himself and still made her believe that
he might be "a frisky one sho' 'nough, if he evah cut
loose." The feelings of the other white males were
plain to her—Vile never took his eyes off her but didn't
have the get-up; Fred wanted her but found it hard
to hit on the right place and time, since she was too
smart to go off alone with him; Abe whacked her some-
times, like a pa, but didn't dare go further; Jed Mar-
shall had all he could do to take care of Nellie, his
young wife, and he'd keep off 'less she, Floh, came
right out and pulled him along; Charlie, a hobo who
had been shanghaied from Libertyville shortly after
John's arrival, made out like he didn't see her but
the back of her head knew different (the prescience of
a young animal). . . .

In her short but intensively skirmishing experience,
men were either attentive—skulkingly or above-board—
or entirely removed, and John's light-worded compan-
ionship left her a piqued perplexity. . . .

One Sunday afternoon toward evening, she loitered
on the road in front of the Vile house and feigned that
she was hunting something in the clumps of blue-
bottles, wild marigolds, and burrs. John had been sit-
ting on a broken-down rocker in the yard—moping
over a week-old Houston paper and wishing he were a
thousand miles away. He hurdled the dilapidated
picket-fence and helped her in the "search," with a
draped smile—claimed to be looking for a brooch when,
if she had really lost it, she'd have known that she
might as well be hunting for a penny in a swamp!

These country girls were certainly dumb in their attempted wiles.

He looked at her indecisively. She was wearing a long, wide-flounced, white cotton dress and high-laced black shoes, and her black hair was greased and waved in a bunch at the back of her head. Her little brown face—blank, and cunning, and aroused by turns—confused him. Didn't want to play with her and get into trouble; didn't care to walk off and feel like a 'fraidy-churl; couldn't help being tempted a little by her spruced-up, warm nearness.

"Let's you and me ramble on down the road aways, huh?"—she looked away and tried to make her face empty as she waited for the reception to what she thought was a daring stroke.

"What for?"

"Foh jimminy-sa-ake, no-othing. Ah jus' reckoned you'd want to stretch youah laigs, 'fraidy-cat."

This aspersion woke him up—he'd show her that she wasn't dealing with a bashful yokel no matter what happened!

"All right, suits me fine." . . .

They walked down the road, and after a mile had been traversed she asserted that she was tired and they sat down beneath a grove of pines. They chatted about odds and ends in their environment—old man Spector's temper; what a fool Ruth Vile was to stand for her husband's beatings; monkey-shines and didos among the negroes—while her resentful doubts increased. If he wasn't plain slow, it must be that this

city fellah thought she wasn't high 'nough fo' hi-im,
but even then it was a puzzlah—no ma-an evah caiahed
'bout high oah low if a gal showed she was set on
him. She leaned against his shoulder and said: "What
yuh thinking 'bout—me?"

"Sure"—the answer was compulsory.

"We-ell, ah'm stahting to b'lieve youah made uh
wo-ood, funny-face!"

He gave her a hard, staring frown—he *was* acting
like a ninny, at that. He kissed and hugged her several
times, and now that she had accomplished her job of
leading him on, she began to struggle a little, but the
struggling was opposed by swirls and dissolvings in her
breast. It felt good to be touched by him—much bet-
ter than she had thought it would—and so she must be
in love with him, and o-oh-h, *let* something dreadful
happen then—she just didn't feel like fighting against
him. As she relaxed against the trunk of a pine, a
revulsion sprang up in the torn middle of his heart—a
long-nursed, scabby grudge against women, as potent
as it was unreal. What had girls ever brought him ex-
cept desertions when he needed them most, and jealous
draggings-down, and wallops, and risks? And here he
was, *as usual*, weakly falling for one he didn't even
think he cared for . . . an under-aged, stupid thing,
who just wanted to use him to satisfy her damned
curiosity and who might lug him into a hellish mess,
if it were ever found out . . . these country-Meth-
odists were always a-aching for a chance to protect their
women

He jumped to his feet.

"Come on, let's go back—it'll be dark 'fore we know it"—he was upset, and scowled to keep his balance.

She stood up slowly, with surprise, stricken vanity, disbelief, and an emotion that tried to be angry but couldn't tighten up enough—the reactions of a simple girl rejected for no apparent reason just as a perilous, long-wooed dream was about to take her.

"What's the mattah?" she asked.

"Oh, nothing, 'cept I thought we'd better trot back in time for supper"—for once in his life he was going to keep out of mischief if he had to run all the way back!

To calm the whirlwind within her, she had to persuade herself that she hated him—so-o, he wanted her to kneel right down and kiss his feet before he'd drop his chin, did he? Lawdie me, she was as good's *him* any day in the yeeah!

"You can jus' slide along and leave me be," she said. "Ah'll nevah have anothah thing tuh do with *you*, 'cause youah jus' a swelled-up lummox, you are! Why say, ah wouldn't walk back with you if ah had to stick heah till the crows picked me clean!"

He begged her to come back with him, with the insistence of common gallantry (that would-be graceful handspring of egotism), but as she kept on throwing epithets at him, he passed into an ill-tempered pride. Let her go to grass then. He hadn't touched her till she taunted him into it and he wasn't to blame for the whole thing, and if she wanted to act like an injured scold, that was her look-out. The maniac within him did not rise because he could understand why she had to word-kick him to maintain her front, but nevertheless, he saw no reason why he should prolong his target-status. Besides, it wasn't nearly dark yet and nothing would happen to her if she walked back alone. After making a last entreaty and receiving another burst of scorn, he strode down the road with a muttered good-by, and she sat down and watched his receding form, with respect, bewonderment, and the sullen desire to retaliate showing successively on her face.

When he had gone a quarter-mile, he found that he had forgotten to take his cap and that a little note-book with a pencil-stub tied to it had evidently slipped from his overalls pocket, but he decided not to re-trace his steps lest she believe that he was looking for an excuse to back down to her. She'd probably bring them back, and if she didn't, he'd go back for them to-morrow. . . .

In the life of human beings, injustice and error often spring from the malicious eagerness with which many men and women snatch at the most inconclusive evidences of wrong-doing on the part of their fellows, as though the first people were forever waiting for the slightest encouragement to leap on some other person. As John slept heavily through the night, he did not know that he was about to experience a ghastly visitation born from the forementioned cause. He woke up when he felt a shaking of his shoulders and heard a loud but indistinct voice. The first minutes of dawn were at hand and Vile was bellowing: "Fo' Gawd's sake, cleeah out uh heeah, Johnny—theyah coming aftah you lickety-split!"

"Coming after *me?* What's the trouble?"—he shook the sleep from him with a shivering bewilderment.

"They claim you done raped Floh Owens!"

"Ra-aped her? Sa-ay, that's a god-damn lie!"

"U-uh-hu-uh? We-ell, theyah gointa swing you up, boy, lie oah no lie. She didn't come back las' night and we found her jus' a while ago, stretched out a mile down the pike. Some bastahd done lammed her on the haid, and ef youah the one, you bettah staht praying to youah Maykah!"

"I tell you I didn't do it, Joe! Honest to God I didn't!"

"Then how come we lit on youah cap and youah note-book raght smack beside her? Ho-ow co-ome?"

"I forgot to take them with me, sure, but I didn't do anything to her. We had a big quarrel 'cause I wouldn't go the limit, and she wouldn't come back with me 'cause she was sore 'bout it, but honest, Joe, I didn't do a single thing to her!"

The woman in Vile believed John against the will of the rest of him, as he scrutinized the other man.

"Mebbe so, mebbe, but that's neethah heeah noah theyah. Ah come back to save youah fool hide 'cause ah know how a gal can get a man plumb cra-azy, and ah come close to being in a jam lak this mahself once. You run out uh heeah while the running's good!"

"Sa-ay, is she dead?"

"Nope, Doc' Plummah ses she'll live but she ain' come to her senses yet."

A fighting scorn took hold of John—damned if he'd scuttle like a chipmunk and imply that he was guilty when he wasn't.

"I'll stay right here where I am. I didn't harm Floh none and I won't act like I did!"

As he spoke, the sound of feet and voices could be heard from the yard. Vile hurried to a corner of the kitchen and snatched up a shotgun.

"All right, ah got tuh make out lak ah came down and covahed you," he said, in a low voice, as he raised the gun halfway to his shoulder and stood still, while Ruth and his son peered in from the adjoining room, with open-mouthed, fear-racked faces.

Ten men burst into the kitchen, headed by Fred, Jed Marshall, and Abe Spector. Each had a shotgun, and a killer's scowl on his face—men who were subconsciously glad of a righteous excuse to be cruel, and conscious-cold with hatred toward an outsider, who had dared to molest one of their women—manacled sexual desires exploding into a dream of virtuous rage. Fred was a tall, tow-headed boy with the small-eyed face of a fairly kindly numbskull now become self-important with anger; Jed, equally tall and with a brown mustache drooping over his lips, had the face of an animal, neither cruel nor kind but ruled by instincts taking advantage of the warped code of ethics donated by his life; while Abe, with his squeezed-in face and stiffly

closed mouth (lips unusually thick for a white man),
was a miser who could be kind sometimes—a sheltered,
holy luxury—but usually sacrificed all objects and
beings to the machine of greed in his heart.

In their assortment of leather boots and leggings,
corduroy trousers, dark blue and tan jumpers, and
dark shirts open at the throat, the men had a clodlike
colorlessness, as they stood in the dim, dingily blocked
and striated kitchen, for neither scene nor costumes
held ought of avenging impressiveness, and only the
guns and twisted-up faces spoke of militant, entrail-
born designs. They paid no heed to John's protesta-
tions, nor did they strike him—to have wasted words
and gestures on a snake would have impeded the busi-
nesslike task of preparing to trample it into the earth
in a more appropriate spot. Binding John's hands be-
hind him with a piece of rope, they hustled him out
of the kitchen and down the road, which was vibrant
with bird-twitterings, insect hummings, and the musky,
serpentine smell of flowers and weeds.

"Where . . . where you taking me?"—John's voice
quavered, and the maniac within him, whose mother
was always the certainty of vile injustice, longed to
rend these men as they were fixing to rend him—an
inner howl in which fear was present but carried out
of itself by the craving to strike back.

These blind dogs, going to hang him for a crime he
didn't do—he'd give his chance of Heaven for just one
minute of free arms and a loaded gun! Jed answered
him, the first time any of them had spoken directly

to John and their first words on the road now, except
for previous monosyllables concerning the need for
despatch.

"Weah toting you raght down to the spot whayah
you jumped on her, you son of a bitch!"

"That's a lie—I never jumped on Floh! I never
harmed a hair on her head"—John barely withheld the
curses rumbling within him.

He'd save these profanities for his last words on
earth—the only brand of words that these men de-
served. . . . The men left the road and stopped under-
neath the tree where John had sat with Floh, and he
smiled nastily—going to string him up right over the
place where he'd restrained himself from taking her—
couldn't be a better joke in a million years!

They hung a loop of rope around his neck and threw
the remainder of the strand over a high tree-branch.
Then Fred climbed the tree and shook the branch, to
test its strength, and as he did, he knocked down a
robin's nest and sent the mother-bird whirring and
circling in the air around the tree, since one of her
eggs was in the nest. The nest fell at Vile's feet and as
he pawed it with his boot, he noticed a scrap of blue-
lined notebook paper with a penciled scrawl on it. Sick
to his stomach and desiring to divert the strain of this
grim business—he could be a petty biter but he was
incapable of supreme viciousness—he picked up the
paper idly and read it several times before the startling
gist nestled clearly in his brain. Then he yelled out:
"Hey, thayah, lookit thi-is, will yuh? Heah's a note

in Floh's haindwriting, shuah's ah'm ba-aw-wn, and looka heeah what it ses: 'Chahlie hit me on mah haid and then he did it to me—F-flo-oh!' "

The others clustered around him and scanned the note—blankness on some of their faces and the lack of a desire to believe on others, since the honey-anticipated killing was too near to permit them to snap back to any degree of reasoning-power, and since the bit of paper, dropping out of nowhere, held a fantastic, flimsily prohibiting aspect to them, and because some of them had reached a pitch where they wanted to slay regardless of whether they were right or wrong.

"Aw, hell, he planted it thayah, that's what!" "How the hell do we know she wrote it?" "Come on, string him up—nevah mind that fool scrap uh paipah!" "Ah'll wagah some niggah pal uh his done sneaked it down heah." "Maybe Vile wrote it hisself—he's always bin soft on the bastahd!"—a riot of exclamations, skepticisms, and cries to hang him anyway, filled the air.

Vile's voice rose above the others.

"You-all listen heah. Ef he stowed that note heeah, oah somebody else did, then why in hell would they put it 'way up in that robin's nest?!"

"The bu-uh-hd done picked it up to make her nest—they didn't figgah on tha-at"—Abe's voice was derisive.

"Ye-es, ah know, but the note's in Floh's haindwriting just the same!"

"Ah ain' so damn shuah 'bout that—note may be a damn fohg'ry fo' all ah know!"

At this moment they heard a horse's hooves on the road and caught sight of Belle, who was perched astride one of the Spectors' plugs. She yelled shrilly at the men, as she leaped from the horse and ran through the underbrush—her little, pale brown, stub-nosed face gasping and tear-specked above the soiled gray wrapper that flounced around the full length of her slim, bare legs.

"Don' hang him, don't hang him," she cried. "He didn't do nothing to pooah Floh . . . he di-idn't . . . he di-idn't!"

Fighting for breath and with a hysteria that approached madness, she dropped to her knees on the leaf- and needle-strewn ground, while the men, actually sledge-struck now, also knelt around her, and John felt that he was already hanging from the tree and just dreaming, dreaming, of a knife that seemed on the verge of cutting the rope while a few last shreds of breath still remained within him.

"Floh . . . Floh . . . done came to her senses jus' now . . . ah swe-ea-ah she did . . . an' she ses . . . she ses it was Cha-ahli-ie . . . Cha-ahli-ie do-one i-it. She ses . . . she ses she come to afthwahds an' then . . . an' then she ses she wrote a note 'bout how he done it to her . . . an' then . . . then she tried hahd to get to her laigs but she jus' couldn't make it . . . aftah she come to her senses down heah . . . and then she fainted way 'gain 'cause her pooah haid was huhting her so much. . . . Honest tuh Gawd, that thayah's *jus'* what she tol' us!"

The evidence was too overwhelming now, and their rage slid to the real culprit with scarcely a jerk of transition. They had no verbal atonements for John —hunt and murder had to be resumed instantly, since a matter of minutes might enable their prey to escape, and John was expected to fathom this exigency and gladly accept his change from a mistaken victim to an avenging member of the posse. Plenty of time for apologies later on. . . . They slipped the rope from his neck, and Abe took his hand and said, "Mighty close sha-ave, Johnny, but it shu-uah looked lak you was the man—shuah did! Come along, we'll all light out aftah the ree-al bastahd now!"

They sped through the underbrush and ran down the road—two of them riding ahead on the horse which Belle had brought—but John sank to the ground and rested on his back, bereft of thought and definite emotion, limply luxuriating in the precious warmth of re-assured life, pressing against the earth as a child might seek the nipples of a mother, who had been remiss in her guardianship. After twenty minutes had flown with the rapidity of gale-driven feathers, the maniac burst into life again, and he sat upright with fists half-clenched and a look on his face so horrible that it could be compared to the visualization of poison-gas. . . . The damn, canker-filled, ignorant, flea-bitten wolves, so anxious to rip a man that they wouldn't stop a minute to debate on his possible innocence unless the sky fell on their heads, and then, when it did, scurrying off with scarcely a word of heart-felt contrition. He'd

love to get even with them—tie up every man-jack
of them and brandish a gun in their faces and make
them believe that they had only a few more minutes
in which to live, and then, one second before their
designated time of death, spit in their faces and release
them with a sneering grin, as though they had suddenly
become too insignificant for him to carry out the
butchery. . . .

Belle had been sitting near him, never taking her
eyes from his prone body and unable to muster enough
assertiveness to stroke him, as she wanted to. Sex
was a tempestuous, forbidding, sinful mystery to her,
and her prodded but untaught heart could only whisper
that she loved him, without knowing why or how, and
then shrink back, fearful of its own temerity. Somehow,
country girls flower into sex and undismayed emo-
tionalism much more swiftly than city maidens between
fourteen and eighteen—possibly because the former
girls are closer to the primitive indifferences of earth,
or because sex is the only fertility present in their lives,
or because the repressions forced on them by their
elders lack the accompanying relief of varied recrea-
tions—theaters, dance-halls, libraries, and fine clothes
—and are therefore much more unendurable.

Belle had been drawn to him day after day—caught
by little things such as the tumble of chestnut hair over
his high forehead; his hands that were long and not
bluntedly gnarled like those of the other men; and
the husky catch in his voice—but she had smothered
the unidentified drummings within her because she was

afraid to listen to them, and out of loyalty to her sister, who was so obviously "making up" to him. Now, as he assumed the light of a wronged, game, invincible hero— hadn't huhd *him* squawking none when she busted in, and raght straight on his laigs too—her feelings toward him took shape, and trembled, and knew not what to do. Physical love—in the graybeard or chickling— when it is not tempered, or instructed by any remonstrances and permissions of thought and more divided emotions—has an elemental surging that is far more mystic than the flesh-withdrawals which spring from anæmia, poorly gainsaid fear, shame, cloying materialism, glorified gall . . . Belle felt as weightless as air, as she slid up to John and took his hand. He looked at her with a hollow, beaten-down, sexless questioning on his face—this was as unreal as the rest of the morning had been. This girl had never noticed him before—she must be just sympathizing with him now. But sympathy from any one in *this* hole on earth was remarkable.

"You pooah chile, they'd have hanged you daid if ah hadn't rid up heah. La-awsie, ah git the shakes 'n' fi-idgets when ah think uh how close you come."

"Well, don't remind me of it"—wasn't a baby and didn't want to be patted, even if he *did* feel the aftermath of a goosefleshy and torn-up heart.

A moment later he reviled himself—this was a fine way to talk to a girl who had just rescued his life, and who was decent enough to be friendlily wrapped up in his feelings now!

"Gee, I'm sorry I spoke so rotten to you—I've been torn to pieces and I don't know what I'm saying. Gee, I couldn't *begin* to thank you for what you did!"

She pressed against his arm and stroked his hair, and he pushed her away gently and with a forlorn approach to a smile on his face.

"See here, Belle, you know I came near getting killed, all on account of your sister shining up to me, you know that. I sure don't want to get into another mess!"

She heard the sounds but their meanings were nil to her—something was buzzing and thudding in her breast: an ungrasped but formlessly autocratic feeling.

"Ah love you, Johnny, honest ah do. Ah nevah come neah you none 'cause Floh was so set on you."

As he regarded her, his surprised and gratified vanity was contradicted by the desire to leave her untouched and not to take advantage of her "baby-dream"—it couldn't be more than that.

"Sa-ay, what do *you* know about love anyway? I'm wise to you, Belle. All you want is to spoon with me 'cause you're wondering how it'll feel. . . . I know."

"Ah know diff'runt. Ah could staind it ef you nevah kissed me all youah bawn days, jus' so's ah could stay with you. . . . Ah'm clean ashamed tuh tell you 'bout it, ah a-am, but ah cain't seem tuh help mahself . . . ah cain't."

Her palpable, head-lowered sincerity—neither gushing nor simulatedly abashed, and free from the fortified moves which he had come to expect from girls of any kind—reminded him a little of Elizabeth's wistful, fewsyllabled directness, and he caressed Belle with the mighty effort to imagine himself back under another tree just beyond Burnside, with all of his spirit still intact and questing.

.   .   .   .

John still stood in his cell and looked at the opening from which the robin had flown. Fifteen seconds had glided on, crammed with remembered motions and motives. Then, a circle of a hemp had threatened to burn into his neck: now, a roasting-contrivance awaited his body. Then, he had been blameless and rushed off in a trice by enflamed, closed-eyed, self-appointed judges: now, controlled, legally sanctioned men, after months of questionnaires, oratories, appeals, and tensions, would give him an approved death—God, he wished they had strung him up then in that cluster of pines. He'd have gone out proudly cursing his tormentors and upheld by a spotless conscience, instead of feeling like a commodity about to be ground up by a vast machine—a commodity still preserving the appearance of a human being and thinking, remembering, with cyclonic speed, to keep from wilting inside. . . .

Since the beginning of this minute, John had been holding an open, silver locket in the palm of his right hand. He lifted it nearer to his face now and looked down at it. It bore the face of a woman, cut from a snapshot, and the face was blurredly smiling in that self-conscious way in which most people greet a camera. Here was a girl whom he hadn't loved, or lingered with, and yet he had preserved her picture in this locket for years, sometimes wearing it beneath his shirt, because she had shown him a quality hard to put a finger on and shiningly exceptional. Noble was a word too bookish and grand to describe this quality; generous didn't quite do it justice; and honest was only a part of it. He let it go afterwards by calling it the whitest and most decent thing he'd ever run into. He remembered his first meeting with her, a little over five years after the cotton-picking days. . . .

Weary of a hobo's life, with its yanked-about subjections, crushing labors, roadside-beds, and skirmishes with melodrama, he had decided to mechanize his spirit, pack up his darkly futile dreams, and give himself to any purgatory, however dull, that could bring him a flexible mattress and yielding pillows; good, varied food; clothes that would let him pass unnoticed; relief from dirt and flesh-scratchings—all of the tangible supports for which civilization exacts such an exorbitant, intangible payment. He had secured a ledger-clerk's job in a large western town near Chicago and had coffined his spirit with rows of figures and percentages—a two-year confinement, broken by extreme dissipations every week-end—women, booze, poker-games where he lost every cent of his wages, or ran up his money to hundreds of dollars. This process of jumping from the coffin, for resurrecting sprees, and snuggling back again with a heavy head, left him more sour, purposeless, and devitalized, but his years of hobo tortures had given him a temporary craving for creature-comforts that had to be slowly sucked dry.

The craving was not the firm symptom of a tame nature but the simmering down of a wild one, slumbering and flesh-dreaming to gather strength again.

When America entered the World War, John promptly enlisted. It was an honorable, applauded escape from the mental ploddings and street-hemmed jags of his existence, and the rightness or wrongness of the war gave him little thought at first. Fighting for his country held a broad loyalty that could not be disregarded, fanned as it was by the clamors and flag-wavings of almost every one, and yet it was not entirely removed from questions and surmises—his country wasn't just the government at Washington, or a symbol named Uncle Sam: it was millions of men and women, most of whom had little or nothing in common with each other, and yet . . . they were all classed as a mutually loving, hurrahing unit. Again, would they become happier in the future through the killing of another country's people? We-ell, no-o, but they had to do it, if their land and homes and the peace of the world were in danger, as everybody claimed they were, and maybe this danger had really brought them together, made them forget the fights among each other and join in a larger one against distantly hostile men.

The possibility of being killed did not disturb him—hadn't he flirted with death in dance-hall scraps, on the rods or blinds of trains on cold nights when his fingers could scarcely keep their hold, along the Texas road, in an automobile crash a year past, when only sheer luck had brought him out with a fractured wrist and bruises? Death was always at hand, war or no war, unless a man went through a veritable pigeon's existence. It was like a race, where death almost caught up to you now and then but couldn't quite touch you until some twist of chance aided it.

If he had reached the trenches and lived through them, he would have returned permanently brutalized and unstrung—the tied-up, largely wordless poet and the relatively selfless muser would have died utterly, with only the flesh-stroker and now scarcely bound maniac remaining. However, a medical examiner found that John's heart was abnormally palpitant—a valvular leakage brought by years of alcohol and nerve-tautness, in spite of his muscular body—and he was shoved into a sergeancy in the Quartermaster's Department at Hoboken, where he kept tab on supplies and supervised their loading into transport-ships. This was a practical resumption of his ledger-clerk's life, except that his mind could rest more while his body benefited from the discipline of early retirings and more arduous work—he could only secure one off-duty night every week and even then he had to be on hand at five-thirty on the next morning, to take the roll-call, so his dissipations became comparatively modest.

In general, he changed to a bystander of life, scanning civilians and soldiers underneath the protection of the first leisure-approaching security that had come to him since his school-boy days and feeling that he wanted to soak up life and understand it better without joining in any of its befuddling wrangles and delights—

a feeling which he translated as "keeping mum and taking it all in." The endless files of profane, horse-playing, dumbly cringing, strutting, burdened, tired soldiers—with here and there a thoughtful, deliberately stoical face popping out from the others—gradually took on a loss of individuality, humanness—flesh, flesh, always in the same uniforms, always packed and hurried on without complaint, or straggling, from any piece of it, and steaming away to kill, or be killed. No man was really different from the other, really aflame with any purpose which he had reasoned out for himself. When you came down to it, most human beings might as well be one man and woman—they moved in a huge gang, and though they fought, or loved, or ignored each other within the gang, all of them walked together in the same direction and made the same mistakes and flurries. Even the rare, thinking faces were swept on with the rest, were little more than faces aware of the ganglike condition and powerless to resist it. What was his own importance, what was the importance of any one man in the scheme of things on this earth? The unanswerable question made him creep farther and farther into the allaying, uncaring, pacified crevices of his being. . . .

But now, returning to John and his remembrance of the girl in the locket, he stood and revived the facets of his first meeting with her. The war had ended two years previous and he was working as a bouncer in a speakeasy in New York City. On one of his nights off he wandered into a dance-hall of the lowest kind, where

independent male-and-female couples and unhired girls
were not admitted. He looked upon places of this kind
as "ninth-rate boob swindling-pots" and yet he dropped
into them now and then because they were depths
where a man could roll and wallow in the sheerest and
most prostrate mud of life and then leave it and cleanse
himself, with the feeling that he had steeped himself
in the worst features of human nature and conduct and
yet overpowered their influence. As cynical as he was,
John wondered how such joints could exist and even
flourish, and he visited them with an abased incredulity.

The hall in question was oblong and high-ceilinged,
with three, large front windows removed two stories
from a noisy business street. A brass-grilled ticket-
booth stood near the entrance, with a brass-railed pas-
sage running beside it—a passage guarded by two,
beefy men who were there to keep out staggering
drunks, men in working clothes, or without light-colored
shirts, and toughs who tried to get in without buying
the dollar's worth of tickets which constituted an ad-
mission. The walls were of light green plaster and
bunches of electric lights, encased by hexagonal shades
of yellow and red, oiled paper, hung from the ceiling.
A wardrobe-checking-room and a stand for cigarettes
and soft drinks reposed in the rear of the hall, and a
band-platform stood in a front corner beside the win-
dows. The five-piece band—cornet, saxophone, trom-
bone, drum, and piano—was composed of men barely
able to obtain entrance into the Musicians' Union, and
they frequently played out of time and strove to con-

ceal their slips with blasts, rackets, and squalls of sound—a merciless profanation of actual jazz-music and execution, which can be paganish and rhythmically foxlike beneath all of its seemingly disorganized wails and knocks. Two sides of the hall were lined with benches where the girls and male patrons sat, though most of the girls stood in a group near the center of the back wall and patiently waited for solicitations, or walked up and down in front of the benches and begged the men to dance with them, sometimes sitting beside a man who seemed easy—neither smartly attired, nor kidding, nor sure of himself—and trying to coax him into dancing by rubbing their knees and shoulders against his, or quickly passing their fingers over his face, in feigned raillery, or squeezing his hand.

Most of these girls were aged between seventeen and twenty-one, though a few of them reached as high as twenty-eight, or thirty. They received half the price of each dance-ticket—five cents—and their earnings depended upon the number of dances they went through each night. Two men stood in the middle of the floor, to tear off part of the tickets and return the other part to the girls, and professedly to see that "immoral" dancing was not perpetrated, though they were blind to everything except couples who rooted themselves on one spot or attempted to violate the privacy of clothes. The male patrons were allowed to smoke and the air was filled with bluish-gray drifts, but the girls had to huddle together and puff at cigarettes in the ladies' wash-room during the five-minute intermissions between dances that came every hour-and-a-half—even mud refuses to rid itself of one or two preposterous soupçons of propriety! . . .

On this particular night, John wanted to observe more than to dance, and none of the girls bothered him as he sat on a bench in The Trocadero, for his clothes —blue serge with trousers wide at the bottom, and a bright tie thickly knotted and dropping from a tight, semi-starched collar of the latest style—and the intent, roving-eyed look on his face, that was disinterested and yet on guard, and the slangy indifferences of his remarks, showed them that he was a wise gazzabo (variation of guy). A girl sat down beside him and for a while they paid no attention to each other, but when five minutes had gone and she still sat there, he noticed the oddity of it. Girls in these places were not given to dawdling and lessening their earnings, except a few minutes before closing time, when they could only make a few cents more and were ready to drop on their feet.

He gave her sidelong looks and saw that she didn't seem to be making a quiet, patient play for him, with arms edging imperceptibly closer and eyes waiting to catch his. If it was a play, then she had it on the most expensive night-club hostess when it came to concealment, but no queen of that kind would be wasting her time in this lowest dump. Really down at the gills and thinking about something, huh? Somehow, these girls seemed to be incapable of any thought except that connected with sexual abjectness, sleeping, eating, and drinking—even much worse than the fleshiest Broadway flip, or the dumbest home-stayer, for the latter women fretted about tasty clothes, or read a cheap book now and then, or paid some slight heed to the events and commotions going on in the world. As for the *emotions* of these Trocadero girls, well, the simplest of jealousies, fawnings, irritations and greeds, were all that they seemed to have. He doubted whether they got much of a punch out of even the gift of their sex, when a man couldn't be worked and they fell for his kidding and his face—even in their nerves they didn't seem to be finely strung enough for wild immersion. . . . Well, if this one was shifting her gray matter, it must be over the room-rent, or a guy who had dropped her flat—something like that—but still, the fact that she was neglecting her business to pore over anything whatsoever made her worthy of attention in this never-slowing flesh-mill!

She had golden hair—the moistly lambent, ferociously heightened yellow-gold produced by hair-wash —and it hung in bobbed ringlets on her head. Her face was long and firm-chinned, with intrenched blue eyes under a low forehead, and a tucked-in, inexpressive mouth. Unlike the other women, with their plasterings of rouge running up to the temples, shellacked lips, and eyebrows frequently shaved and always blackened, she used only a moderate amount of cosmetics and avoided the razor. Her body was near to stoutness but its lack of abrupt curves kept it from being gross, and she was wearing a low-necked, orchid-mousseline dress and black pumps. H-hmm, looked just a wee bit classier than the others, and she'd been through the mill too— the lines on her face told him that she must be at least twenty-eight. Another five minutes flew and she still stared ahead of her and even refused the tickets of two men—a procedure which, when observed, brought a girl beratings and then dismissal in The Trocadero, for the girls were ordered to dance with anything that had two legs and didn't bite. The last action made John open his eyes—no other Trocadero girl would have done that in a hundred years unless she was too sick to stand up, or awaiting the immediate arrival of a steady customer.

"What's eating you, baby?" he asked.

"What's it your business?"

"Fall off and die—can't a guy ask you a question?"

"Sure, keep on asking."

"Say, you've wandered into the wrong joint. There's a taxi downstairs waiting to take you over to the Ritz-more Roof. You're wasting your ice in this boiler."

She looked more closely at him—not too hard on the eyes, and his line was more Broadwayish than those of the roughs, laborers, and paunchy business-men who thronged The Trocadero. Still, any fellow could pick up a line without being so mu-uchy-mu-uch.

"Well, you can take your sign down 'cause I haven't been peddling any to you."

"Ye-eah? Well, here's a tip. If you don't want a fellow to talk to you, put some cottonwool in your ears and stay out of cheap dance-halls. The combination might work."

She smiled in spite of herself—a smooth kidder and wise to the night-life works, no doubt about that. Might be a hoofer, or bootlegger, who had floated in out of curiosity.

"Don't make me laugh—it's bad on the tonsils."

"Cut them out and have a good time, girlie."

"You'll pay the doctor, I suppose."

"No, thanks, I never pay myself. I get it from others."

"You don't think *much* of yourself, do you?"

"Stop talking in your sleep—it might be contagious."

She chuckled at this and said: "I guess you know your onions, Jack."

"Biggest crop of the season—have a few on me and then tell me why you were acting like the last rose of summer."

"What's your drift?"

"Listen, whenever a girl in this joint sits on her fanny for ten minutes and turns a couple of guys down, it's time to call in the undertaker. What's on your mind?"

"You're getting personal, you are."

"Tell me something I don't know. There's no glue on *this* bench and if you want me to stop chinning, just move along, girlie."

His hard and yet interested manner, and his immunity to jabs, convinced her of his class now, and she started to thaw out.

"Don't get sore now. A girl's got to know who she's talking to."

"Well, size me up and get it over with."

"Aw, I know you're k.o.—it's all right with me."

"Then stop sparring and tell me what's on your chest. Maybe you're a new one here and the smell's getting your nose."

"Naw, I've been here since February, all through the summer, but I'm sick and tired of it. I can stand just so much and no more."

"Took you a long time before your stomach turned, didn't it?"

"Well, what can a girl do when she's lean on coin and she has to go out and raise it?"

"This isn't the only graft on earth."

"No, but I haven't got no special talent and I don't see how a shop-girl or a steno's got much to brag about either. You got to take what comes when you're down in the world."

"Twisting your hips off and rubbing a bunch of grease-necks, huh? You're mighty dumb if you can't land anything better than that."

"So I'm *dumb* then. What do you do that makes you so wonderful?"

"Me? Just a bouncer in a speakeasy up in the Forties, but I don't have to lie down and take the leather anyway. Why, say, I've seen all of them, high and low, but I've never spotted a joint quite as raw as this one!"

"You said it there, and you don't know the half of it. This joint is so bad it'll turn green some day."

"Then why not get out of it?"

"Ye-e-eah? Well, just get me a better job and watch me run."

"Maybe I will—I was born on Good Friday."

"Yeah, I know, just too good to li-i-ive."

"Sure, that's what they all say till I slap them down. If you want me to help you, girlie, don't kid so much."

"I won't, Jack, if you don't want me to."

"I'm not handing out any orders—just talk regular and forget your line. I might get you a hat-checking job in a swell night-club I know, if you take your high hat off."

"Say, are you on the level about this?"

"Nothing but."

At this juncture one of the Trocadero owners—a large-bellied, short man, coatless and wearing a flashy silk shirt below his shaved, flatly rapacious face—surveyed Betty Mason, the woman to whom John had been talking, and said: "Say, girlie, what's the matter with your feet to-night? Bunions or something? If you want to take the night off, you come to me first."

"Well, if I want to park here *I'm* the loser and nobody else."

"Oh, yeah? With a crowd of guys here on a Friday night and six of you girls staying away, huh? Think again, bright-eyes, think again!"

"A-all ri-ight, keep your collar on," John said, as he

rose to his feet. "I'll take care of her tickets, don't worry about that."

The owner looked him over and decided to go slow.

"You've got me wrong," he answered. "I'm running a dance-hall, and I've got to see that my patrons are satisfied, that's all."

He turned away and John fox-trotted off with Betty. He liked the way in which she had talked back to the owner—he had watched the other girls do everything but drop in front of the man—and though she had sometimes reverted to the usual smooth-rubbing chatter, it hadn't been half as bad as the crap most of them handed out, and her sense of humor had worked full speed. He'd take her out after closing-time here, if she didn't claim to be dated up, and see what she'd try to pull. Maybe she was a straight one—one in every five thousand get that way, to paraphrase a street-car ad.

Betty, who had lurched through everything from street pick-ups to the entertainment of brokers and minor politicians, was at present snarled up with a squad of underworld men, who sometimes used her as a stall-moll in their thieving rackets, and though she saw no chance of breaking away from them, she always told herself that she *might* be able to shake them with the help of a two-fisted, on-the-inside fellow, who could give them cold feet when they came after her. She was on the boundary-line between stupidity and modest intelligence—able to see her broad situation but unable to contend against it. Her heart was juvenile and blas-

phemous in a continuous allegro rhythm that swung her
to profanely physical sprawlings at one end and dreams
of respectable, refined, tenderly sheltered happiness at
the other. She was cravenlike in the presence of male
beatings and intimidations, and yet she had the poten-
tialities of super-courage, which were liable to shoot
forth at any moment if she were goaded too far. Her
virtual captors sensed this latter spark and handled
her gingerly during the occasional times when she
merely scowled and said nothing—"she's a soft dame
when yuh got her on the run, but she ain't a broad yuh
c'n monkey too much with."

In her early twenties, she had lived decently in a
house in the Bronx, with a widowed mother and a
younger sister, and had worked as a manicurist and
gone out with plain working-boys of the neighborhood,
but when her mother died and her sister married and
moved to another city, she became overjoyed at this
freedom from home-restraints and determined "to have
the time of her sweet life" and play men without com-
ing across to them. Over-sexed, and not nearly the
"wisenheimer" that she thought she was—in tricks that
could gratify her passion for lazing around and fineries
—she had soon passed from one man to another, ex-
cusing the transition on the ground that there was no
other way of getting by—the heavy-sugar men wanted
a girl to treat them on the very first night, and the
willing pikers were not worth chasing, and the men who
were knock-outs and knew it wouldn't stand for any
stalling on a girl's part, and besides, it was hard not

to fall for the last kind—a girl was only human. . . .

The gang that she was tacitly hooked to—badger-game men and small-fry friskers—kept her at the dance-hall because it was a good blind and she could furnish them with occasional suckers among the patrons. As the night wore on, she lost her vague intention of trapping his roll and became really attracted to him— he seemed to know the ropes from top to bottom and yet he was a nice kiddo with nothing nasty about him, and also, he probably had a tough crowd of his own, if he was a speakeasy bouncer, and she'd get mixed up in shooting if she let her mob take him, or cleaned him herself.

After 1 a.m., he took her to the speakeasy where he worked. One of her cronies had been standing near the street-entrance to the hall, but a wink of her eyes had turned him away. She and John sat in the basement-haven crowded with loud-tongued actors, touts, ticket-sharks, girls living on men but denying it, male touchers forever out of a job but always on the edge of getting one, gold-diggers handing half of the spoils to a master behind the curtain, virtuous schemers looking for a sugar-papa husband, men living on fatuous women, dolled-up gangsters with perfect manners and murder in their fingers, prosy business-men playing with fire to become less prosy to themselves, professional yes-men, embryo-eyed kibitzers, perverts trying not to reveal their spirits but slipping into the "Bert Savoy" vernacular with each succeeding glass— the minor motley rabble of Broadway. It would take another book to describe them in all of their smears, vagaries, and frustrations, and they are incidental in the remembrance of this condemned man standing in his cell and staring down at a locket. . . .

After the eighth highball on each side, Betty became utterly carnal, unfencing, and almost childlike in her giggles and invitations, with her subconscious self pouring through the "wise" top veneer, and John, shrugging his shoulders inwardly, and yet keeping an eye peeled for male trailers, or any overt action on her part, took her to his hotel-room, where he stood in with a clerk, who became blind on such occasions—the old finale, stamped and wrapped up, but one that most people, from dish-washer to minister, craved like blazes in spite of all their masks and moral spiels. Funny, this healthy appetite on one side and lying squeamishness on the other—almost like people hated themselves and were out to kick their own happiness in the pants while still sneaking to it behind the locked doors.

He rested on the bed with her and felt enervated— even sex was losing its flame and becoming a moderate, almost-despised necessity, clung to because it was about the only importance he had. All his past dreams of expressing himself—if he used an express-company now, he certainly couldn't insure his mental packages for much—and doing things that would set him apart from the rank-and-file, and rising in the world, and finding a woman he could trust and kneel to, a woman who would understand what was going on inside his head—what a senseless joke they'd become. Just born with a load in his heart and no way of spilling it out. While he was far from being cultured, he could talk straight and only semi-burdened English when he chose to, and speaking out of the unconscious depths of his mood, he began to drop his protective slangs and treat Betty as an equal. In spite of her mental limitations, she carried an ignoramus's admiration for education—'guys who were as tough as they made them, but could drop it and show how brainy they was, when a girl got to know them—fellows just reeking with class but able to take care of themselves under any circumstances.' She warmed up to John and told him about the inside of the dance-hall, and despite all of his sophistications and murky knowledge, he was nevertheless rasped by some of her revelations. After all, Broadway used perfumes, side-steppings, and declarations of good-fellowship, to cover up its messiness; and the real underworld was an understandable menagerie, but The Trocadero had them skinned a mile when it came to vapid dirtiness—not the censor's idea of dirt but every degree of ill-will, flaccidness, surreptitious pandering, and abysmal deceit. Somehow, as he listened to her, the last shreds of illusion and visioning fell from his being, and sex became a beautiful thing—the thing it had been with Elizabeth under that tree—turned to destroying dross by the fears and machinations of humans.

Her recital, condensed and qualified a little to ap-

pease the warped, self-holy sightlessness of our censors,
goes as follows: *

"The girls who get the most tickets have to go the
limit—roll their hips and stomach and let a guy grip
their legs between his, or bend them back till they'd
have to be contortionists to go any farther, but the
guys wait till they get to a corner of the floor . . .
don't do so much of it out in the middle of the hall.
The fellows wouldn't care where they did it but the
bosses tell them: 'Not out here, bo!' . . . To rake in
the tickets a girl's got to stand for more too—pinching,
and cheek-kissing, and thumbing. Some fellows won't
dance with a girl unless she promises to go out with
them after one o'clock, and lots of girls make dates
with five or six men for the same night, and then they
scrap over her out on the sidewalk afterwards. . . .
Three of the girls have got husbands who live off them,
and the husbands come down to the dance-hall ev'ry
other night and watch their wives shake and twist on
the floor, and tell them to hop to it and bring in the
coin. When the cappers on the floor—the men who
tear the tickets—get a crush on a girl and she won't
tumble, they swear to the boss that she's holding out
on the tickets, or getting too free, and too free in this
joint means doing everything bu-u-ut, so then she gets
canned. . . . A gang of Italian toughs hangs out at
the hall and when a girl stands them up, or she won't
do what they want, they beat her something terrible.

---

* A case-history from an actual dance-hall girl in Chicago.

Sometimes they'll go right up to a bench in the hall
and slap her, and all the bosses do is take them aside
and tell them to air their troubles on the street—
'don't crash her face he-ere: d'yuh wanna get us
ra-aided?' The system is not to bother the rough
babies but made a big show of taking up for the girls
by going after the boobs and the silly-looking peanuts.
When a sap tries to manhandle a girl, the-en they rush
him out on his ear. F'r instance, fellows aren't allowed
to smoke when they're dancing, but the wops get away
with it and the other fellows get it in the neck. The
other night a Spanish fellow was dancing and drawing
at a nail—it was his first time at the hall and he didn't
know about the rule, and besides, that joint wouldn't
give a fellow the idea that he had to tone himself
down any. Ed, one of the cappers, walked up and
jerked the cig from his mouth and swore at him. Well,
of course, no fellow with the least guts will stand for
being treated like that! Still, all the Span' did was
ask Ed why he didn't tell him to stop 'stead of jerking
his pill away. That's all, but the next thing he knew,
they lugged him out to the hall and played jazz-drum
on his face. . . . Some of the girls live in rooming-
houses and take guys up there but most of them have
got a boy-friend on the side, and they try to work the
customers for a good time, and big tips, without going
the route with them. Some of them are in with crooks,
but then the girl always manages it so's the guy gets
cleaned *after* he's left them, so's they can't be blamed
for it unless he squawks to the cops, and most of the

time he's dead drunk when it happens and he can't even remember where it was pulled, or what the cleaners looked like. . . . A few of the girls are decent and live at home, but they might as well not be when you think of what they have to put up with on the floor—there isn't much lacking. The bosses don't actually force a girl to stay with them—they don't have to 'cause there's enough girls only too glad to be good to them and acting like the bosses was ma-ayor, or something. But just the same, if a girl don't yes them to death in the hall, they always cook up an excuse to can her. Ev'ry now and then one of the bosses gets on the band-platform and bawls the girls out for standing in one spot on the floor and ses he'll drop the next one he catches doing it, but it's nothing but a play to the gallery, of course, and it gives him an opening for getting rid of new girls who don't suit him—girls that act a little ladylike. A little's enough to get the bum's rush in that joint! Why, they even tell a girl to wear as little as possible under her evening-rags. That's the whole system—bluff like the devil and then close their eyes. . . . I've seen some pretty square girls come to the hall, but if they don't quit after a week or two, they start to get smutty and careless. When the girls flock into the wash-room during the intermissions, the wisest person on earth would be surprised at some of the stunts and jokes *they* pull off. . . . A girl gets a mean idea down at The Troc'—she thinks she has to take abuse from a few guys 'cause they've got the whiphand over her, so she takes her

spite out on the other fellows and lies to them and
plays them for all they're worth, and then she feels
sorta like she's revenged herself. It's the same way
with the men down there—some of them act sweet
and decent to the girls at first, but after they've been
gypped and fooled a few times they turn rotten and
try to put over a few tricks on their own hook. . . .
I'd like to have the mazuma the bosses pay over to
the cops—a grand a month is chicken-feed. The cops'll
raid a joint that caters to Filipinos, and Japs, and
Chinks, because the higher-ups and the papers raise
a howl about that, but otherwise, if a hall is closed
you can bet your last leaf it was because it wouldn't
pay enough. If there's a investigation on, the halls
just get more strict and stop half of the raw stuff till
things quiet down again. . . . I'm a long ways from
being straight and I've stood for a lot in my time, but
I can't stomach that joint any longer. It'll make me
throw up if I stay there another week!" . . .

Feeling utterly disgusted with sex and life, John
plied Betty with whisky until she stretched out in a
stupor and then he turned his back on her and stared
up at the door-transom for an hour—barren, unmov-
ing, and suicidal in his heart—before he fell into an
ogrishly dreaming sleep. . . . When Betty woke up
on the next morning she was muddled about what had
transpired in the room except that she remembered
she'd poured out a tale of woe to him—God, she hoped
she hadn't blabbed about her connection with Red

Hurley and the mob!—and she took it for granted that she had come across, and felt peeved—what did a woman get out of it when she was too stewed to know what was going on? She assumed the stresses and confidences of a mistress and tried to make him amorous. He treated her with a persistent coldness, which she misunderstood. Thought he was the gravy and better than she was now that he'd had her! She'd been k.o. for a spicy night when he wasn't dated with somebody else, but now he wanted to shoo her away and trip to some younger, prettier girl, whom he could bulldoze and show off.

Well, maybe she could get him to make another date, *and if she could,* we-ell, her gang would take him down several pegs, the puffy-chested speakeasy bouncer! If he had been a man to whom she had yielded only for his money, or a designated sucker who had somehow managed to turn the tables on her, she would have been unaffected by his seeming scorn, or departure, but here she had really felt a crush on a man after knowing him only a few hours—not a violent one but so-so at that—and he was paying her back by freezing her out on the very next morning. It just went to show that a girl had to keep her head or get the dirty end every time. Women of her kind become so limping-souled, blackguarded, prosaic, and blackmailed, on the top, that they distrust not only the man but their own emotions too, and yet the difference in Betty that made her an individual was that she would have clung to John despite terrific odds if he had proved insistently

loving and had not apparently rejected her now—the
pang for unseduced, profoundly voluntary emotion and
mutual respect between herself and a man, which
stirred beneath all the refuse in her heart and would
not quite die.

When he agreed to meet her on the night after the
coming one, her shrewishly retaliatory mood wavered
for a minute—after all, maybe he was the sort that
slowly got fonder of a girl, instead of raising the roof
the first week and then fading out—but the reaction
came to grief because her entire past life said "no!",
and because he still acted in a hand-restrained, friendly
manner which she construed to be coldness. She wasn't
a twenty-year-old flapper any more—couldn't believe
in a guy just on the chance that he might back it
up. . . .

He met her a little after 1 a.m. on the appointed
night, and after they had hopped into the taxi and he
had told the man to drive to a speakeasy, she said:
"Say, big boy, how about coming up to my flat?"

"What's the bright idea?"

"Aw, I'm fagged out to-night—just haven't got pep
enough to step out now. You come up to my place—
I've got a vic' and some real rye and ev'ry thing.
Come on, Johnny."

"Yeah? Who's paying for the layout?"

"Never mind *who*—*he* won't be there to-night. Not
a chance in a thousand."

"How d'you know he won't?"

" 'Cause he went to Boston this morning—hope to die if he didn't."

Ordinarily, John would have scented a game and told the girl to forget about it, but he was still in the throes of a befouled, unclad mood, rare even to his penchant for blackness, and she hadn't sprung anything in the wind-up of the first night, and who in hell cared—he'd throw the money in her face, if that was what she was up to! They rode on in silence for another two minutes, after she had directed the driver to go to a number near lower Tenth Avenue, and the far-off frown on his face gave her a chill. Maybe he was wise and had a gat on him—no use feeling his hip pockets, for that would make him suspicious, if he wasn't already, and besides, he might have a small one inside his coat. Simply to make conversation, she asked: "Listen, why'd you slip me that frozen mit the morning 'fore last, after you'd had a good party with me?"

"Ha-ad nothing. You passed out and then I went to sleep—never layed a hand on you."

She examined him closely now—it must be a lie, but what for? He wasn't a fat-head by any means and he sure knew that he couldn't gain anything by posing as one.

"Go-o o-on, tie the animal outside," she said. "You must think I just left home, to pull that stuff."

He became irritated now—they were so damn leery it was a wonder they didn't try to cut their own shad-

ows off, and yet they acted like they expected a man
to swallow anything they handed out.

"Left home? You're about two steps from the door
right now. You're so used to tinhorn sports you just
can't believe that any man could keep his paws off
you. If you want it straight, here it is. That inside-
dope you gave me about The Troc' made me so damn
sick of women that I wouldn't have touched you if
you'd been Peggy Joyce herself. I'm a pretty wise
bird all right, but the info' you handed me was enough
to make a guy run to the doctor!"

She tried to disbelieve him, but the drive behind his
words was too real, too smashing—no fellow could put
on an act like that unless he was Barrymore himself.
No, he hadn't grabbed her and she didn't have a single
reason to be sore at him—this sure turned everything
upside-down!

"Gee, I got it all wrong," she said, and then, after a
pause: "But say, why'd you meet me to-night, then?"

" 'Cause I've made up my mind to stick with you, if
you've got the same idea. You're certainly no worse
than the other broads I know, and I've got a hunch
that you might show an honest streak if a fellow
brought it out of you."

Now she felt dynamited and softly in pieces. She'd
played the game for years, and she wasn't a mark for
anybody, but Chri-ist, she liked this fellow—liked him
more than she'd ever guessed until now—and he be-
lieved in her in spite of the fact that he didn't trust
other girls—not a sap's ignorant belief but that of an

experienced guy, who saw something fine and decent in her. And now, here she was, leading him to Red and the mob 'cause he had a little roll on him—no, she couldn't be that rotten, couldn't do it to save her life.

Just as she reached this conclusion, the cab stopped in front of a three-story rooming-house. To have backed out now would have meant exposing the whole thing and having him turn on her with his dukes, and she wouldn't blame him either. Confused and shaken, she let him pay the driver and walked into the hallway with him. What was the answer? What? . . . Straining for a loophole, she decided to tell the fellows he had nothing but a "v" on him and it wouldn't pay to empty him that night, and that she'd save him for a night when he was heavy and tell him that her fictitious papa had suddenly come back from Boston and everything was off. She told him to wait beside the front door because she wanted to go into the first-floor parlor alone and make sure that her sugar hadn't returned. He smelled something decayed then, and after she had entered the dimly lit parlor he hurried outside and stood on the walk. Ought to beat it now, but unless there was a mob they couldn't do much out here, where he'd have a running start on them.

After a lapse of five minutes, she came hurrying down the stairs and said, in a quick, low voice: "Come on, Johnny, we'll run down to Tenth and grab a cab. I'll tell you what's up afterwards. Come on, ple-ease."

Curious now, he hastened down the street with her, taking care to look behind him every few seconds.

They hailed a cab on the Tenth Avenue corner, and as he stepped into it, he looked back and saw three men standing on the stoop of the house to which she had led him. Everything was clear now except the running-out and escape, and as they rode on, he extracted the pitifully sordid-sacrificial facts from her.

After discovering that he hadn't taken her and then tried to give her the cold shoulder, as she had thought, and after realizing that she was too soft on him to carry out the game, she had whispered her story of postponement to Red Hurley, and his two pals, who were standing behind the portières in front of her rear bed. She hadn't been able to repress all of her nervousness though, and they had suspected that she was covering up her faltering and had ordered her to bring him in, or they'd make it hot for her. Then, to gain time, she had acquiesced and told them that she might have to string him along for a minute or two, if he had smelled something rotten and gone out on the steps, since she knew that they wouldn't immediately peek out of the window and risk being seen by him. . . .

When she had finished the tale and was cowering in a corner of the cab, spent and unable to turn her head toward him, the maniac broke within him and he punched her in the face, and then checked himself as the situation dawned on him—this girl had placed her life in jeopardy and let herself in for a hunted future, or at the least a thorough beating, just to keep a gang of two-by-four crooks from jumping on him. A positive

miracle. He looked at her with alternations of aston-
ishment and self-berating on his face.

"Jesus Christ but I'm sorry I hit you! I just couldn't
get it into my dome at first. . . . Sa-ay, you're as
game and white as they make them!"

"That's all right, I had it coming to me"—her voice
was barely audible, as she straightened up and rubbed
the swelling bruise on the side of her cheek.

He looped her with his arms and they kissed for the
next few minutes. Then she asked him to stop the cab
at a corner drug-store because she wanted some lini-
ment for her face, and when he started to follow her
out of the cab, she told him that it would be silly for
both of them to leave, since she'd only be gone a min-
ute or two, and that the hack-driver might think that
they were trying to escape from paying him. Too over-
wrought and air-treading now to grasp the possible
significance of her departure, he settled back in the
cab and waited. After ten minutes had passed without
her reappearance, he snapped back to reality and hur-
ried into the drug-store and found that she had disap-
peared—through the side door, undoubtedly. . . . He
never saw her again, but afterwards he found that she
had slipped the silver locket into one of his coat
pockets.

.   .   .   .

Standing in his cell, which now became a stone and
metal sentinel of death, whose firmness and strength
prevented the quarry from escaping, John sighed, and
his sigh was a last, pain-borrowed, dazedly affectionate,

unbelieving-in-death stroking of life. Life, despite all
of its quarrels, surfeits, ponderous misleadings, cor-
rodings, and quandaries, was idiotically dear and
warm, so indelibly, sweetly warm that his entire body
revolted against leaving it. Just the feeling that you
could rise from a bed again and pit your heart, mind,
and flesh against those of other human beings, no mat-
ter how hopeless, or betrayed, this pitting might be;
just the ever-planning security centered in breathing
and the moving of arms and legs: just the knowledge
that reviving surprise, though the odds were a thou-
sand to one against it, might nevertheless tap you in
the midst of your grayest sinking: just the fatuity of
telling yourself that each day was never quite like the
other. Here was his will-to-live, furnished with better
adjectives in this description, perhaps, but a veracious
rendering nevertheless. If he had been a few seconds
removed from killing himself, unbearable despair, or
weariness already a living tomb, would have turned
life to coldness, but no man about to be slain by others
—regardless of what morbidities and defeats he may
have had—can ever attain quite the heedless cleaving
that comes from voluntary choice.

John placed the silver locket on the table—let them
find it after his death: they didn't know her and it
would be meaningless to anybody else, and all of its
value would depart with him, since he alone held the
secret of this value. He raised a piece of paper and
read it. . . . "I'm not sorry or glad that I killed her
—I'm just hoping that we can meet again and explain

things to each other. She was mean and she had no dreams, but maybe those things don't matter after people are dead. John Musselman." . . . Afterwards, the newspapers were to flaunt this note and call it calloused, and childish, and an unsportsmanlike attack on the dead woman, and they were also to comment on its lack of religious repentance—in the small-souled, time-serving fashion of most modern papers—and he guessed something of this as he held the paper in his hand. No, they wouldn't like this note, the dumb-sisters and jackals who'd print it and buzz about it to-morrow, but it wouldn't be unanimous—some few people would understand and hope that he'd get his wish if souls were really in bodies. Yes, the world did have just a few straight-brained, self-candid, deeply scanning men and women, with hearts as wide as the sky and almost no hard prejudices in them, and they were one of the main reasons why he dreaded to die now, but they were so obscurely sprinkled over the face of the earth that it was impossible to reach more than two or three of them during a lifetime.

He thought of the dead woman and his experiences with her—he had been saving her as a farewell to un-pleasantness and compassion; a slowly falling salute to the selfishnesses and frenzies of life; a dreamily battered, fathomless, calm-eyed reconciling of thought to the illy-paid madnesses of flesh; a final emotional contact with the ruinations and boiling-over sordidness that life could hold. The injustice-hating maniac within him, which had struck at flesh because it could not reach the less tangible source of goading unfairness and yet craved to destroy this basis, had now subsided to the most discredited of flutterings. Life had been the sustenance of this maniac, and now that death was only an ominous inch away, it evaporated into breath-panicky uselessness.

John had met the now-dead woman well over three years after his demolishing episode with Betty—met her through a flirtation flippant and common enough during the first few minutes, but suddenly leading to newness and belabored attention. He had been walking in Central Park, on an autumn afternoon—one of those afternoons when great islands of bluish-white clouds approach the myth of the horizon with wind-driven swiftness, and equally great clearings of sky in between gleam with the impenetrable detachment of a concave ocean defying gravity, and the sun dodges and reappears, like a blinding monster, diving beneath the islands and rising to breathe again. The trees had a jubilee of crimson and orange, the close-clipped lawns were flecked with dry brown, and the strength-less lashings of the air were inciting but did not hurt. To the east and west, huddled apartment-buildings and hotels jutted into the sky, and their uneven, flat-topped, pointed roof-lines epitomized the ambitions of a city, where the beginnings of height end in hard desistings; where the gradations between individuality are in-finitely irregular and yet compressed into a small range; and where the practical compromise of angles reigns everywhere, with more imaginative and dauntless

curves and circles limited to flesh and its diversions
in theaters and jazz-palaces. . . .

John walked along in a dissenting mood. He was
stale and gleaned-out after a gin-swigging night, which
had ended in the arms of a chorus-girl, whose chat-
tering cupidities had been washed away by alcohol,
leaving nothing but gurglings of carnality followed by
the terror and spite of a six-year-old, who had been
inveigled into neglecting her little gold dollie . . . stale
and depleted, and yet the autumn day was too unfor-
gettably bracing, too slapping and booming with pro-
fuse mellowness for his mood to hold out against it,
and smilelets soon simmered at the corners of his
mouth. It was a boon just to be alive on a day like
this, just to squelch every atom of the past and let
the sun, wind, and trees make your spirit as tall and
playful as they were. . . . One whopping fault in
people was that they didn't hug the earth and rub it
into them and sit for hours under a tree and do nothing
but stretch their hearts and minds, and get still for a
while without caring who loved or hated them, or how
much money they had—earth, not mud with slime on
it and not the dirt formed in houses and on streets.
People lived as far away from the ground as they could,
and covered and shielded themselves in every way to
keep the sun from their skins, and stamped their hearts
and muscles out to earn the little comforts that doped
everything but their senses. If they'd only flock back
to the earth—not like those Texas farmers, or hill-
billies he'd seen during his hoboings—on the earth but

not a part of it and using it only to wrest a living out of and acting in between their labors much like city people who had grown much less sophisticated during a lifetime vacation—but like men and women who wanted to dream and rest, and feel a cleaner fever, and work barely enough to give themselves clothes, roof, and food of a plain kind. . . .

Fine ideas, with last night's gin still stinking in his breath. Like thousands of them, he took it out in chinning to himself and wishing, when he'd knocked against another sore spot in the game of swilling, chasing broads, and matching his muscles and tactics against those of insincerely smiling, or obstreperous men. The city was a poison that got to a person and yet made him believe that he was a smart leader in some particular crowd and having the time of his life—to nightlife people along the Bulb-Lane it was figurative heroin and physical variety; to householders in the Bronx and Flushing it was near-beer, with a chaser of whisky sometimes on the side; and to those in the slums it was bad booze, coca-cola, week-end movies, and cheap vaudeville. . . . These were *his* thoughts—not the author's—an explanation caused by revered critics, who persist in confusing the author with his main character of the same sex and asserting that he is completely in accord with this written character's deductions and spirit merely because the creator has shown a large sympathy with the struggles of this semi-fictitious man, or woman. . . .

One conclusion stopped the conflict within John—

he was at the end of his youth now and unless he exerted
a last strength to bound out of his rut, save up money,
and take a shack out in the country with some simple-
minded but loyal girl, he'd become more and more
reckless and wind up as a nickel-grafting, dribbling
soak, or die with his shoes on. Starting this week, he'd
stow away all the money he could put his hands on
and in about a year's time, if luck was with him and
he cut his booze down, he'd be out in the country for
the rest of his life. He let his thoughts become aim-
less now, and they reverted back to the chorus-girl
of his past night . . . a girl brought up by another
fellow to a wild party in a flat in the Seventies—con-
sidered wild by the participants (and by observing
literary critics!) because they dropped some of their
clothes and verbal lies and forgot money, prestige, and
mind-panderings for a few raucously inflated hours—
and then losing her escort for John, with the usual fist-
swinging avoided by the fellow's eventual gin-stupor.
God, they were only themselves when they were drunk
—take this girl, straightly sullen as a kid who'd made
up her mind to have a gorgeous feast in the pantry,
and sticking there because his mouth was jam-sweet
to her, and then waking up the next morning with a
grouch, and: "I hope you don't think I'm the kind of
girl that makes a *practice* of this," and a fret to get
back to a phony tale to some man, and asking for a
sawbuck to pay her landlady and furious when he
wouldn't give it to her because he knew she wasn't up
against it. God, they were nothing but sex and even

that was corrupted and gypping unless they drank too much!

He dropped on a bench and continued his inveighings against the sex-lure that repulsed and yet enmeshed him —knew what most of them were and raved to himself against their cheapness, but fell for them just the same. If there was a consistent bone in his body, he had yet to locate it! The trouble was that a man became starved without sex and had to accept it for what it was and what people made it, or else feel like an unmasculine spectator, and besides, you could try like hell but you couldn't quite kill your hope that a fine, stimulating, harmonious, bottomless mating of impulse and thought would visit you again in the shape of some unique woman. A perfect cynic would need to be cross-eyed, locked up, and impotent!

A woman sat down on the other end of the bench, and since plenty of empty benches stood nearby and most women were not in the habit of selecting one occupied by a strange male, if they could avoid it, John spied a possible play and squinted at her with an interest just a figment above indifference—he didn't have to stalk them in Central Park, not this year. She was wearing a cloche-hat of simple blue felt, skull-fitting and with a becoming tilting of lines that indicated price, and a knee-length, dark blue dress of cashmere and a black coat generously trimmed with kolinsky at the cuffs and collar. She had a small, dimpled face, colored with that dissolving of olive, gray, and pale brown that has no language-label, and bearing just a skillful taint of powder and rouge, but no lip-stick—a face that just now seemed too imperturbably vain to be actively bored, and too sacred to itself to permit the surroundings to intrude: a face that held green eyes, selfishly curbed, small lips, and a straight, wide-nostriled nose below auburn-brown hair and above a slim-slender body of medium height.

As John took her in his interest mounted several notches. *Looked* the part of a society girl around twenty-eight—scores of actresses, chorines, and kept-babies dressed in good taste and tried to look oh just too weary to exist, but they *invariably* smeared the war-regalia on their faces, and this one didn't. A society girl would hardly be apt to stroll in the park and flop on a man's bench, ha-ardly, but if this woman was a veiled hooker, she wasn't an ordinary one unless appearances were a joke. . . . It would be a joke now to chin with her and have her turn out to be a cashier in the Automat, or a hotel-manicurist. He'd lived long enough to know that you couldn't tell anything about them until they opened their mouths and even then, six times out of ten, you couldn't be positive till you took them out. Not that he cared whether she was a cashier, or a celebrity, or a scrub woman—he left the snob-stuff to those whose spines couldn't stand up under the load of what they really thought about themselves—but the laugh rested in the fact that clothes and a far-off stare could make any broad seem like Mrs. Astor's daughter.

She gave him covert, expert glances and assured

herself that he was not too old, not badly dressed, or groomed, and friendly to her concept of handsomeness —outside of those things she didn't care whether he was a crook, or a shoe clerk, since she had sallied forth with the vague intention of allowing a presentable man to talk to her, *if* he proved to be not too forward, or too instantly impatient with his hands, or too conversationally impossible. There wouldn't be much risk in the broad daylight of a park with policemen and other men near at hand—most males were overjoyed when they had a chance to pose as gallant saints, or D'Artagnans, and rescue a woman from the "foul grip" of some other male.

Two nights previous, at a gathering, she had become sentimentally democratic over her fifth cocktail and declared that women in her circle never really saw life, and unpolished, swearing men, and that it wouldn't hurt them just to walk out on the street alone some night and see what happened to them, if they kept their wits. In a drawing-room, night-club, or Harlem Black and Tan, a woman witnessed only what was dished up to the sightseer and she never ran into really shady, awkward, exciting, side-splitting people and things. After she had been laughingly advised to visit a movie called "The Streets of New York," playing at the Strand; to finance a whisper-low and be the power behind the yells; to learn how to operate an airplane; and to rent a studio in Greenwich Village, somebody had piped up that he'd triple-dare her to take a jaunt through Central Park and scoop in a decent-looking man—he had a wonderful powder that would cure the headache she'd get, and influence enough to keep her name out of the papers after her newly acquired friend started to punch her in the eye. Unserious but just a wee bit nettled, she had asserted that she'd take up his dare and that she wouldn't need his after-assistance either—any woman who retained a cool head and wasn't a believing child could handle the worst man on earth! . . .

She had forgotten the repartee on the next morning, but on the present afternoon—with a suddenly canceled tea-engagement emptying her hours until seven and with a mood suspended between delinquent self-weariness and shoulder-shrugging—it had risen again in her head. Oh, take a walk in the park and *look* at some of the males anyway. Nothing startling would happen, of course—at the most a little, screamingly amusing talk with a conceited traveling salesman, or actor out of work, and then the promise to meet him at nine on such-and-such a street corner, which she wouldn't dream of keeping—but it would be a trifling divertissement and the autumn air would do her good. She was neither a nymphomaniac nor an undiscriminating coquette, but her sex was uninvaded, lightly stuffed without being pierced, alert to clinkings and brushings of vanity that left her still supercilious and self-contained, and fickle in a nibbling and then retreating fashion. She had never loved or hated deeply and she was incapable of these emotions—marooned on an inaccessible isle with the man perfectly suited to her conscious taste

—one who spoke rarely but trenchantly (in her opinion), and abused and waited on her by turns whenever she signaled without actual words, and had a cold but carnal heart and a darkly strong face and body— she would have thrown herself into utter sex with him for a month and then subsided to a complete lack of response, and dismal, animal-trapped boredom. She had only enough self-awareness to enable her to nag herself into honesty when the other person seemed to be overwhelmingly hurt, or deceived, and to push herself into manifestations of culture—critic-worshiped books, plays, and music that could lend a chatting, modernly stenciled assumption of knowledge to her lightly sense-ridden interior: and just enough conscience to wish that she were less selfish, during times when other people's veiled accusations grew in volume and couldn't be circumvented, though afterwards she forgot the matter by telling herself that her accusers were even worse than she, if the truth were known.

She could be kind, in a listless and deliberate way, when the cost was far from draining and incessant, and she was almost totally devoid of jealousy and envy, since people and objects were not compelling enough to agitate her. She could also be horribly cruel without realizing it, without considering it more than another skipping-on, or retirement, in the hide-and-go-seek sport that nearly all people engaged in, except in the dully warm security and taken-for-granted affection of their rôles as husbands, wives, fathers, mothers, sisters, and brothers, and even there, very occasional deviations and neglects were only human. To her, men and women said "I love you," and then jilted each other afterwards, without being blameworthy, or wittingly insincere, and without becoming greatly cut up about it unless they were of the very young, very dramatically susceptible kind.

She could be abysmally petty in her self-enveloped effervescences without, in her own opinion, doing more than protecting herself against the real pettiness of other persons—they *would* be, if one didn't scheme and evade a little—and yet she could shift to an idle generosity when slight self-doubts made her need to pat herself on the back. Her husband had died two years previous—a man whom she had neither loved nor detested but found endurable except in his cups—and the experienced but unshaken sex within her was now in a mood where it wanted to branch out and see if it couldn't be roused by men outside of the well-mannered, carefully manipulated, correctly twitting ones whom she knew—men who would be rougher and slyer, and make her step more swiftly to evade their lunges . . . might even *take* one of them, if he could set her on edge physically, but only for a short time, of course. She had descended to her father's summer chauffeur once—a broad-shouldered college boy with a lisp and a ukulele—and another time she'd had a secret night with a clerk in her uncle's brokerage office—a youth who had been stupid, good-looking in a Valentinoish way, and flatteringly infatuated with her—but these men hadn't been quite unrefined, or street-

levelish, or unscrupulous. Just for a heaven-sent
cha-a-ange, a brute, or an adventurer, might give her
hitherto unknown whippings of spirit and flesh.

She was living with her parents now in a four-story
stone house in the Eighties, just off Fifth Avenue, and
wealth and luxury were appendages too solidly habitual
to her for any more attention than that given to the
floor under her feet, and she was at present romping
about with men who did no more than caress her just
up to the danger-point when they were full of cocktails,
or speak of the sacred delights of marriage and never-
dying love—a once-pleasing skirmish, which had now
become more thrill-less, especially since the routines of
her ended marriage-life had made her light sexual ap-
petite unaccustomed to lengthy abstainings. . . .

In any description she would seem slightly unreal
because she was unreal to herself and because she had
never flung herself against the least sharpness, commo-
tion, stench, travail, or snare of life—a curiously un-
singed, never-still, self-sustaining combination of moth
and flesh-dabbler in human form, despite her twenty-
eight years. Women of her species were partly vic-
timized by their childhood days. Already coolly sexed
and perceptibly over-selfish then—selfish in the blind,
measured, dream-slain way that has nothing to do with
morals, or fables of sacrifice—they became petted,
sterilely cloistered, anointed and artificialized until
their traits attained an abnormal fixity. . . .

John had a whim to discard the old reliables and

make a remark with some meaning to it, just because he didn't care whether she walked off, or not.

"It's a beautiful day to wash off the dirt of last night's gin, isn't it?"

She turned and stared—*this* one started off originally.

"To-o wh-at?"

"I think I said wash it off. . . . Don't mind me. I get a little crazy in the head sometimes."

"That's a remarkable way of opening a conversation."

"Just as good's any other."

"Are you sure?"

"Reas'nably."

Now she'd say something to disconcert him.

"By the way, are you fli-irting with me or trying to make me lead a better life?"

"Yeah, I'm flirting with you, if you mean we're both killing time. The second crack's easy too. When I find out what a better life is I'll start to spread the gospel, but I haven't struck it yet."

This one "didn't disconcert," but hit back good-naturedly and talked fairly decent English and didn't say what he was expected to—charming, go on.

"You know, I'm convinced you're an expert judge of human nature—just *knew* I wouldn't be impressed by the usual remarks."

He grinned—an educated devil of a kidder, huh?

"Don't be convinced the first two minutes, girlie—it might get you in bad—and don't think I'm trying to impress you either. I'll manage to live if you can't fall for me."

Gi-irl-li-ie, wasn't that *immense?* And he was rude
without much of a sting, and self-possessed, and
straightforward—at least his technique held all of these
qualities. Perhaps she'd stumbled upon a man of some
importance in the theatrical or night-club world—a
teacher, or a mildly well-bred business-man, doctor,
lawyer, would never have said girlie. Somehow they
just wouldn't. However, it would be entertaining to
draw him out and test him some more—"good, clean
fun," as the village comedian said.

"Then I suppose you're just talking to yourself—
sort of al-lo-owi-ing me to be present."

"No, I'm not Mayor of New York this year, so I
don't a-allo-ow people. You'll stick around long's I'm
interesting to you, but I'm not out to make a hit with
you."

"No?"

"No is right. I'm talking to see what you're like,
and you've been kidding and trying to measure *me* up.
That's all."

His bluntness was refreshing to her—didn't he seem
to have a veritable *passion* for frankness? Decidedly,
an eccentric man with fresh impacts, so far. She'd keep
up her spoofing just a while longer, to see if she couldn't
somehow make him faltering, or unable to answer, since
she wasn't used to being stopped short like *this*.

"Are you sure you are not the Mayor's *secretary?*—
you talk so decisively. Really, you seem to read people
at a gla-a-ance."

He smiled tolerantly—she was determined to razz

him, probably to see whether he'd get ill-tempered or swing at a low ball, but he could play this inning till New Year's Eve! A high-grade, clever, upstage girl, and one that he had always wanted to meet—one who was accomplished in ways outside of coin-dredging, sex-peddling, hoofing, and jazz-bawling, and who knew the fine points of the language and could make him spin his tongue off to keep pace with her. He'd been introduced to such girls in night-clubs, but they were giving most of the private-telephone stuff to their escorts, and in that atmosphere they drew on the slang because they thought it was an initiation-fee and caused them to be accepted as one of the crowd.

"We haven't been doing any reading *yet*. We've just been razzing the first page of the books, girlie."

"What did you find on *my* page?"

"Well, let's see. Guess it would go something like this: 'Uh, leaving her Mole's-Choice in the platinum garage invented by her father, she ankled over to Central Park and' . . . how's it go here? . . . oh, yeah, 'and for want of something better to do, she sat down. She met a strange fellow and she put her high hat on, but it was a breezy afternoon, very breezy, and she had some job to keep the lid from blowing off.' How's that for a starter?"

She laughed—her thin, brief trill of a laugh, in which mirth always planned the next step—and decided that he was rich in vitamins and should be assimilated in large portions. Regardless of who he was, he was hilarious, and odd, and nobody's fool. She talked more

seriously to him and found that he had ideas on people
and life that were fumbling-tongued and sometimes
dera-anged, but fresh and truculently appealing to her
—like a combination of a Coney Island freak-show
and Carl Sandburg at his worst, in her opinion. She
asked him what he thought of books, music, paintings—
Edith Wharton, Dreiser, Strauss, Stravinsky, Cézanne,
Van Gogh—and he confessed that he knew nothing of
these people but had always wanted to run up against
their work—it was hard to know where to start, or how
to cope with their lingo, or where to find people who
talked about them. Working in speakeasys and night-
clubs, in a life where he never reached his bed until
dawn, he had to sleep into the early afternoon and then
wake up with a brick in his head and a rotten disposi-
tion. He did read a "highbrow" book now and then
—one that the newspaper-reviews called a knockout—
but those books never gave life as he saw it. They
overlooked, or toned down, the meanness and dirt; or
they yawned at people's sufferings; or they had a lot
to say about how vulgar and stupid most business-
men were, when everybody knew it except the men
themselves (and what good would it do *them?*); or
they spun their stuff out to three hundred and fifty
pages when it could have been said in half the space;
or they were hopeful and romantic as hell, but didn't
back it up with any sound arguments; or they dug into
people that lived in comfortable homes, and raised a
pile of dust about whether they should take each other's
bodies, or they shouldn't—sex was a main part of life,

sure, but it wasn't gilded over, and drawn-out, and suffocated with politeness, and there were other things behind it that *they* never mentioned. Of course, he had no right to pose as a critic, and he might be all wrong, but he'd have to stick to these beliefs and feelings until he met some one able to change his slant —some one who knew much more than he did. He looked wistfully at her, after this last statement, as though he were beckoning to her "classiness."

His last outburst brought her dilly-dallyings of playfulness, patronizing, surprise, and airy scorn—imagine this sporty roughneck inveighing against the lauded novels of his time!—and yet this very audacity was exceptional in a man of his rank, who practically never cared to investigate anything except wages, jazz-music, and the next woman. In literature and art she docilely followed the "reputable" and most-read critics of her day—wading through books that she didn't like, because they had been recommended as powerful, authentic, and poignant, and looking upon more radical works as circuses, to be laughed at if she could understand parts of them. Her mind was far less intelligent than John's, but supplied with hundreds of patters, words unknown to him, borrowed dismissals, and informations, which he mistook for a radiant superiority. God, he'd been waiting years for a girl like this one— the woman that Elizabeth might be now, if she'd had the leisure to investigate the beautiful and serious things in life—who would have the ability to break up and correct his entire existence, if he could only hang

on to her! But what in hell did he have to give *her?*
We-e-ell, maybe she would fall strong for him just
because he was so utterly different from what she was—
because he'd be a royal shake-up to her and teach her
the inside of his world while still eager to learn hers
. . . take another sniff, Johnny . . . it was only dope.
For all he knew she might really be a society girl, who
had wanted to amaze herself by doing something daring
and speaking to a strange man—she had none of the
tactics, earmarks of any hooker he'd ever seen—and in
that case he'd have as much chance with her as a last
year's gag on Broadway. Again, she might be the un-
usually bright kept-woman, or wife, of a rich man, or
shady guy in the heart-swing of the city's night-stir,
and what would he have for her then? . . . Plain sex
was his only hope, he guessed—a physical kick that
would draw her to him in spite of the difference in
breeding and intelligence. After all, he'd seen the
dumbest muts with the smartest broads, and vice versa,
and money didn't always explain it. Sometimes there
was only one person at a time who could get breast-to-
breast with them and make them wild about it, no
matter what that person might be otherwise . . . a
dizzy, tripping-up, real and yet semi-invisible attraction
that nobody could explain, not even the persons them-
selves. . . .

She made up her mind to have a gorgeous, skin-
exhilarated but secretly unmoved, condescending, dis-
guised fling with him. Just sex, and a delicious lady-
ship over his ignorances—he wasn't by any means a

real fool but just uncultured, uninformed—and the tang of the rough love-making he would probably stage, with all of it supported by the knowledge that she could instantly disappear the moment he wearied her, without the explanations and re-meetings that might be necessities with a man of her own circle. When did people ever succeed in explaining the miserable advent of boredom?—they were either inexhaustible reservoirs to each other, or shallowly enjoyable for a time, but they could never be positive concerning which was which. . . . He was a barbarian pure and simple and yet he had grotesque, pathetic, home-made aspirations to climb into an appreciation of higher things— a riotous, distracting contrast, which she certainly hadn't bumped into before, and for the rest, he was reasonably handsome, well-groomed, and his manners might not be utterly impossible—not at all a bad bargain, and one with a new touch of spice within it. Of course, she wouldn't break his heart by leaving him— her own novelty would wear off after a while and he'd probably be tickled pink to return to other girlies, as he called them, who'd be more admiring and easier to understand.

She gave him an assumed name, Helen Proctor— her real name was Frances Hemmingway—and told him that she lived in a flat in Washington Heights and that she was the daughter of a college professor and had taught English in a high-school until her bad health had forced her to take a long vacation. He neither believed nor disbelieved her, but felt that he didn't care what she was—a college-graduate standing behind some counter or a rich man's pet—as long as he could meet her again. If she was chained up to a jealous man, or a mob of high-powered racketeers, there'd be hell to pay if he kept on going out with her, but he was used to that danger and he couldn't die more than once—life, when you boiled it down, was one endless fight to get things that other guys wanted too. It was a muddy, hitting-under-the-belt, ugly free-for-all, but he couldn't change it and wasn't responsible for it—he'd been thrown in head first and had to make the best of it. To keep himself a little more honest and searching and restrained than most of the people he knew was all that he could accomplish, and even that was a mighty difficult job sometimes. . . .

She agreed to meet him two nights after the approaching one, in a small restaurant in the Forties near Broadway, and then, to keep her address hidden, she let him walk with her to a subway-entrance and stood downstairs, near the change-booth, for a few minutes, before ascending to the street and hailing a cab. . . . He wasn't at all sure that she would show up at the appointed hour—she might have taken him for a ride, to air her good opinion of herself, or it might have been her idea of a pleasantly harmless adventure before she leathered back to the man she was nutty about—and the morbidly apathetic poise of his past three years became shattered by this possible mockery of a fancy, brainy, easily-looked-at girl flitting through his life, for an afternoon, and making it doubly hard

for him to trudge back to the rank-and-file of her sex.
He groaned at the one-sided, willful refusals of life—
stupid girls, decent as the word went, loved a man and
clung to him in the hope that he'd marry them, and
ordinary diggers handed him their favors after they
had imbibed too many highballs to remember their
game, while a rare, intelligent doll with class down to
her toes strung him along on a bench and then trotted
off to her master—a man who might not even appre-
ciate her gifts. . . . Unreachable unfairness (trans-
lated by him to the phrase: "a low deal") . . . almost
tempted a man to throw in the sponge sometimes.

When he caught sight of her in the little Italian
eating-place, he felt like a tight-rope walker back on
the platform again after nearly slipping during his per-
formance . . . felt ashamed of his complaining pes-
simisms . . . felt disarmed, renewed, and on edge
. . . felt a less substantial restoration of the Burnside
boy hacking its way back through fourteen years of
deaths and hardenings. The sentimentalist within him,
so often blasted, starved, baited, and forced into self-
derision, since his Elizabeth days, and so often reduced
to feeding on figurative morsels—the re-creation under
the pine-trees, the self-transcension of a beaten-down
dance-hall girl, and tenderly selfless flashes from women
who became stiltedly commonplace when daylight
brought them back to sanity—raised itself for a last
grapple with slippery needs and visions . . . yes, last,
since a man cannot drag on the weight of poisoned
hopes forever, and since his thirty-two years had left

him only enough emotional energy for one more dream, one more attempted flight from street-scheming averages, one more concession to 'faith and the seeming closure of ruptured happiness.

She was dressed in pleated, ochre organdy underneath a tan evening-wrap, without a hat, and her small-lipped, green-eyed face held a peculiar expression—a little of the cat dreaming that it was a mouse and waking up for half-unidentified moments, though to herself, she was only welcoming a sexy, semi-gauche, stooping-down interlude and teasing it to see what surprises and humors it might hold. Whether she'd see him again would depend on to-night—if he broke loose and tried to dominate her without becoming positively boorish, it would be delicious, but if he passed into pleadings and rubbed-out compliments, she'd say bye-bye without his knowing it.

After the first amenities, he persisted in talking about books and their relation to life—subjects which he hadn't had a chance to converse on for years, except to himself—and dutifully, she gave him reviewer's clichés, which were gems of thought to him because they had adjectives and nouns he had never heard before—baroque, rollicking, rococo, arresting (he knew this word only in connection with policemen), dynamic, vital, experimentalist, denominator, preciosity—and she basked in his earnest respect. After two years of study and exhaustive reading, he would have roared at her present remarks—for his mind was not unreceptive but merely hesitant in a field where he knew so little—

but now they seemed to be gloriously astute revelations. Then, when the meal had ended and they were sampling the bootleggers' version of chianti wine, she rebelled against the discussion—she hadn't come down to deliver a lecture on novels to a man whose objections to this author and that were humorous but absolutely idiotic.

She steered the talk to a more personal basis, to see if he would fawn on her as so many males did.

"You haven't paid me a single compliment to-night . . . do you feel sleepy?"

"If I did, I'd sure wake up after *that* brickbat. You know you're pretty, and I don't know yet how it feels to kiss you, and I'm not much on peddling bouquets."

"Feels to *kiss* me?—I must say, you're taking a lot for granted."

"I just said I didn't know. When I try it you can hand me the verdict then."

"But suppose I tell you I don't want you to try it?"

"That'll be jake with me. Nobody can struggle with a woman and make her love him—that's apple-juice. If she wants him she'll get weak in his arms, and if she doesn't, he'd better say nightie-night."

"My, how you've got everything di-ia-agra-amed. It must be marvelous to feel so certain about things."

"That's right, keep on kidding—I'm used to it. The only time people ever get serious about sex is when they're plastered, or when, well, when they're so goofy about each other they can't help it."

"Perhaps I am in love with you, um, pardon me, go-o-ofy about you. How do you know?"

"I'll bite—how *do* I know? No objections to your telling me though."

"But, my dear boy, the calendar won't permit it—it isn't Leap Year."

"Yeah? People le-e-eap any day in the month if they're really gone on each other."

"But you haven't told me whether you care for me."

"That's so—I'm terribly absent-minded to-night. All right, here's the breathless news. I'm not quite in love with you, but it wouldn't take much of a push to get me there."

"Dear me, do you always take so long to make up your mind?"

"Long? Say, a couple of nights must be a lifetime to you."

No woman had the slightest use for a man if he let her walk on him, and as much as he was beginning to care for this endlessly teasing, covered-up girl, she'd have to drop her false-face before *he'd* say a word more than he had. She laughed at his last sally and remarked: "I'm beginning to think you're the most unromantic person I've ever met. You bother so much about time, and pushes, and other silly things."

"Yeah? Well, I could have the same opinion about you. You haven't even told me whether you like me or not."

"Of course I like you, silly, or I wouldn't have come here."

"How much?"

"We-ell, you remember what you said about push-ing, don't you?"

He smiled and stroked her hand over the white table-cloth—he'd win this girl, or break two legs: marry her too, if he could. He was accurate enough in his ratings of other women—actresses, spade-wielders in the golden garden, working-girls, country lasses—whose general characteristics he knew from experi-ence, and in their regard the elements of uncertainty and contradiction could be held to a minimum, but Helen was a new creature to him, with her contrast of sheathed sarcasms and soft invitings, each side sheering so gracefully into the other—to him—that to save his life he couldn't tell just how inwardly serious she was.

He had induced a friend to substitute for him that night—he was working as the door-custodian in a club near Broadway—and he wanted to take her to this hang-out, where there was no chance of being gypped in the bill, but she refused to go because it was a place sometimes patronized by people in her crowd, and so she pretended to dislike this particular haunt. They rode to another place, which had a grandiloquent French name, and glass-topped tables with gold-fish swimming underneath, and every color-shade in the spectrum on the walls, and a smoothly demented jazz-band conducted by the worldly, tune-clever son of a millionaire.

Celebrities and well-known hacks hung out at this

club and they could be spotted at the different tables—
an over-fat, dark-skinned, feminine blues-shouter,
whose laughter stopped for a few seconds out of every
ten minutes and then continued like a steam-siren; a
tall blond columnist for the *Evening Traffic,* who sat
collecting indelicate gossip, cheap innuendoes and musty
gags for his scandal-yelling sheet; a paunchy, bald
movie-magnate, who was forever nudging his pretty
companion and picking his teeth; a musical-comedy
star, whose Semitic, near-ugly face was fanciless but
jovially honest; and a novelist-playwright—a kinky-
haired, would-be devilish-faced man, who had just
startled Broadway with a newspaper drama of hyper-
bolic stenography, in which the characters spoke like
blends of slimy satyrs and undressed truck-drivers on
a stag-party. Frances had once said "how-do-you-do"
to the novelist-playwright, at a soirée, and she made
John take a corner table where she would be moder-
ately safe from recognition—some one walking up and
saying: "Good evening, Miss Hemmingway," would
make her dear barbarian frightfully suspicious. He
delighted her because he was challenging and out-
spoken and yet had a longing for her that prevented
the challenge from becoming harsh, and because he
could exhibit a boyish penitence which gave the lie to
his often slangy jeerings, and because he could put
over his admiration without flatterings and self-lower-
ings, and because she sensed that he could be a tempest
when his heart was really touched. The smaller mat-
ters were nicely adjusted, too—he didn't look out of

place in his Tuxedo, and his table-manners weren't half as bad as she had expected them to be, and his dancing was a gliding dre-e-eam. If there was a single reason for not having an affair with him—for a week or two anyway—she couldn't spy it, except moral ones, of course, and they were things that most people voiced on the outside and violated whenever courage and opportunity came together.

When she grew tipsy, with a man who attracted her intensely, she always became sentimental in a woe-begonely effusive way—enormous selfishness reduced to its fundamental lack of bravery and meekly glorify-ing it—and self-deprecating, and unnaturally wistful to the point of babyishness. Her thin, flitting, un-wounded sexual desires became intent on imagining themselves to be firm and maddened then, and she seemed to lose every sign of her former twittings and coynesses.

After John's hip-flask was empty, she leaned over the table and said: "You're a darling, darling bo-oysie, really, you a-are."

"Don't come so fast—I might believe you."

"But I me-e-ean it. I'm not teasing a bit now."

"How do I know you're not? You haven't said you loved me, have you?"

"I do love you, Johnny-boy—I think you're the sweetest, o-oddest man I've ever met."

"Do you mean it?"

"Yes, of course I do."

His heart became leaping and ignited now. God, how

he wanted to believe, how he hoped that it wouldn't
be just another physical night—this one or the next—
with dullness and good-by showing up in the morning
light. He had had sessions of that kind with plenty of
girls but he hadn't loved them—the past trio excepted!
—and their departures had only added hair's-breadths
to his hopelessness. Now, it would crush him down if
she ever left him . . . he knew.

"Oh, I know, maybe you're crazy about me *to-night,*
maybe, but how d'you know it'll last?"

"Oh, look at this ma-an, will you—poking around
for re-easo-ons when there a-aren't a-any. I'll love you
for the rest of my life, I'm perfectly sure about it."

"I wish you was as sure as I am, 'cause I'm in love
with you for keeps."

"I wo-onde-er."

"Well, don't."

A pause came and then she said: "I'm so-o tired of
sitting here, darling. Let's go off somewhere and be all
alone with each other . . . anywhere . . . I don't
care."

He rose from the table and as she stood up too,
his heart slid into a singing, convulsive dream—that
dream which is so saccharinely unreal, or fleshily
stripped, to the outsider, but which is all of escape
that we may know—a dream that was to be the final
one of his life.

• • • • • • •

Thus began an affair which endured for two weeks,
and included three meetings in his rooming-house abode

—meetings that revitalized over two-thirds of his faith in human beings, and gave substance to the tentatively returned boy within him, and dumped years of searing cynicism out of him, and gave him an emotion that was not bashfulness but a fear that the least bungling misstep might destroy the precarious structure of his happiness. The acquired traits of cynicism and sophistication exist in two varieties. The first is never more than a coat of mail resting upon an adverse sensitivity, but the second is evolved from an innate acidity and, through a process of years, resolves itself to the permanency of skin. John's embittered skepticisms had never been more than compulsions wrought by the deceits and greeds of other people, and now he threw them aside, with only a twinge of hesitation. . . . 'Aw hell, if you couldn't believe the words of *one* human being out of the whole pack, then it was time to call it an evening!' Helen said that she loved him and he'd better let it go at that—he had the damn habit of always wanting to poison his own happiness. . . .

It is never safe to generalize about a condition as individualized and crisscrossed as love, but when this condition is not a night-born lust and when it is experienced by the oppressed, dying youth of a man who has idealized it in spite of every no, every foulness, it seems to defy psychology—to take on a mysticism that flaunts every slowness and dissent of logical interpretation. Then, sneering prostitutes become blindfolded infants; boys and girls kill themselves; sleek businessmen change to "verse-writing" drivelers; old women take on the simpering blushes of seventeen; gunmen act like Saint Anthonys; practical grubbers stumblingly approach an elated lyricism—and the world only snickers, or weeps, or turns another page of Keyserling and Havelock Ellis. . . .

John completely lost his critical faculties and pardoned, or enshrined, every word and action from Helen. When she made a remark too purposeless, inane, for even his deafness to ignore, he told himself that she was simply trying to descend to his level; when she was self-possessed and distant-eyed while he embraced her, he felt certain that it was caused by a past, unfortunate love-affair, which had left her distrustful of her own heart as well as his, and to which her memory sometimes reverted in the midst of his caresses; when she seemed to have a petty motive, he accused himself of maligning her and expecting her to be inhumanly perfect; and when she flew into an ill-temper, he shouldered the blame and rebuked himself for being an annoying clod sometimes. She promised to marry him —he was so insistent and so delightfully moral about it, and if it would pet his conscience during these few days, why not? A night-club bouncer with some pretense of a moral conscience was too delicious a phenomenon not to be encouraged, though she told him that he would have to wait until she sounded her parents out, since they had a dreadful opinion of Broadway men and would rave if they knew that she was in love with him.

After each meeting, she left him during the early

hours of the morning and talked him into letting her go home alone in a cab—'it would be ridiculous for him to ride away out to Washington Heights and then back again, and she'd be happy with the knowledge that he was getting some much-needed sleep instead of returning to his room just before dawn, and she could catch a machine on the corner, just a few steps away from the rooming-house.' . . .

Toward the end of their third meeting, as she sat in his dully-tinted, bric-à-brac-cluttered, front parlor— with its brass bed behind dark portières, and spindly, curved-legged table, and ugly, black leather and oak chairs—she yawned to herself for the sixth time and felt immeasurably prosaic down to the tiniest crevices in her evenly beating heart, and a little degraded—not in a moral sense but in that of a vanity which had stooped too low to snatch up a bizarre conquest. She smiled coldly at her present position—a smile in which her sex, almost angry at its present satiation, charged this weariness to a ludicrous, past blindness and thrill-chasing. What on earth was she doing in this hideous, spotty room, with a simple-minded, vehement, adoring nonentity sitting near her? She had been positively insane to give herself in the first place, and it was high time that she came to her senses and acted like a twenty-eight-year-old, normal, discriminating woman of the world. She could scarcely believe that this episode had *ever* been new, or exciting, to her—it had undoubtedly sprung from a whim to see what it would be like to have an affair with a forceful, candid fool, and from too many highballs, and an inexplicable dementia in her head.

As she rose to her feet, she intended to make another engagement with him and break it—he didn't know where to locate her and she could go down to Palm Beach for a month and make sure that he wouldn't pester her, if he accidentally discovered her address and status—but a whim of consideration interfered, since her selfishness was a trifle uneasy despite its determinations. Oh, why shouldn't she be truthful for once in her life—even if such lies were forced upon her, to escape from expostulations and "tearful" farewells—and part with this man in a friendly manner, instead of making him sit two hours in a restaurant and wonder what was wrong? Of course, he'd been making a weird, furious drama out of it, just as she had, and he'd protest a little, curse a little, and then kiss her good-by and trot off to his other bro-oads, as he called them.

After she had adjusted her hat, she turned from the mirror and said: "Well, it's been a nice little party, hasn't it, Johnny-boy? Of course, it just *couldn't* last forever."

He stood erect and stared at her—the words were alarmingly careless, but so entirely opposite to her past ones that he couldn't immediately accept the edge of their meaning.

"Nice little pa-a-arty? What's the idea?"

"O-oh, don't be so tra-agic about it."

"About wha-at?"

"Not seeing each other again, of course."

He stepped closer to her and said: "Say, listen—don't kid me now, please. I'm not in the mood for it."

She sighed—why did they *always* act like the Dying Gaul and then forget about it when another pretty girl treated them sweetly?—her method of counteracting the mounting uneasiness and foreboding in her breast.

"I'm not joking with you, Johnny-boy—I'm just being delightfully honest for a change. . . . We've both been playing with each other and having a perfectly glorious time, but it's lasted long enough now and there's no reason on earth why we can't remain the best of friends, even if we *don't* see each other again."

"But you said you was going to marry me"—the naïve, whipped, Burnside boy making his last gasp.

"Of course I did, and neither one of us meant a word of it. Don't act like a si-ix-ye-ear-o-old-chi-ild when I know you're nothing of the kind."

He stood in front of her and gripped her shoulder.

"See here, Helen, d'you love me, or don't you?"

The "histrionics" were beginning to bore her now, despite the warning murmur in her bosom, and she removed his hand and walked toward the door, before turning.

"No, I don't, if you *must* keep on acting. I'm practically engaged to be married to somebody else, and you'll probably be chasing another girl the minute I leave you."

"Sa-ay, I'll bet that Washington Heights story was a damn lie too!"

She became angry now—she certainly wouldn't allow herself to be profanely reprimanded by a man who wanted to soothe his pin-pricked vanity. If she had admitted to herself the slightest possibility of the fact that she had cruelly and irreparably hurt him, her entire egotistical structure would have fallen down upon her head and crushed her.

"Of course it was, and now I'm going to leave, since you *can't* talk decently to me!"

As she closed the door behind her, a black typhoon ravaged his heart until the heart-tissue, to him, seemed on the verge of splitting open. He caught her in the hallway and dragged her back to the room. She screamed once, but his fist, driving against her face, silenced her voice. A liberated maniac now, he choked and beat her for a full ten minutes, as he knelt beside her prostrate body and cursed her. Then he leaned back against the wall and stared down at her, hour after hour, with all of his heart and mind dazed, empty, and incredulous, and all of his body motionless.

. . . . . .

The Lutheran minister, a portly, broad-faced, flat-nosed man, looked at John with a stunned, transported mixture of compassion, and immersion in a distant God, whom he sought to appease with the despairing flight of his prayers. Then he tugged at John's arm, and together they intoned the sentences: "But thou hast in love to my soul delivered it from the pit of corruption. For thou hast cast all my sins behind thy back." Then, with the minister stepping behind him, John strode out of the cell to the waiting guards—a living corpse, whose little, funny, jerking steps were all that remained of life.

THE END